SYLVAN T. RUNKEL

CITIZEN OF THE NATURAL WORLD

BY LARRY A. STONE AND JON W. STRAVERS

Edited by Cindy Howell
Layout and design by Karisa Runkel

Turkey River Environmental Expressions
Printed on recycled paper with 20% post-consumer waste content

THANKS!

Publication of *Sylvan T. Runkel: Citizen of the Natural World*
was made possible in part by donations to a Sylvan Runkel fund established
by the Iowa Natural Heritage Foundation. The statewide, member-supported
organization builds partnerships and educates Iowans to protect our natural
resources "for those who follow." For information, contact INHF
at 505 Fifth Avenue, Suite 444, Des Moines, IA 50309-2321;
phone 1-800-475-1846; www.inhf.org .

IOWA
NATURAL HERITAGE
FOUNDATION
"FOR THOSE WHO FOLLOW"

The Iowa Association of Naturalists also awarded a financial grant
to aid in the Runkel biography project. IAN is a nonprofit organization
of professionals and volunteers who are actively involved in interpreting
natural and cultural resources in Iowa and in developing interpretation skills
and educational programs. For more information, contact IAN at 2473 160th
Road, Guthrie Center, IA 50115; phone 641-747-8383; www.ianpage.20m.com .

Iowa
Association of
Naturalists

Printed in the United States of America
Published by: Turkey River Environmental Expressions
23312 295th St.
Elkader, IA 52043

ISBN 0-9729441-0-9

Sylvan T. Runkel
CITIZEN OF THE NATURAL WORLD

CONTENTS

ACKNOWLEDGEMENTS

When we undertook this biography project, we were overwhelmed by the number of people who eagerly agreed to tell their stories of Sylvan Runkel and who offered the use of photographs. That in itself is a tribute to Sylvan. Of course, special thanks must go to his family for their patience and cooperation and for offering insights into their beloved husband, father, brother, grandfather, and great-grandfather.

Bernie Runkel shared her home, her food, and the happy memories of her 42 years as Sylvan's partner, wife, and mother of their three children. And she provided access to Sylvan's huge collection of papers, books, photos, and memorabilia.

Geneva Runkel Henss, Sylvan's sister, displayed a boundless Runkel energy and enthusiasm as she contributed recollections and photos of the family's heritage and her childhood with Sylvan. Geneva adored her big brother and loves to talk of his life and accomplishments.

Son Ramon Runkel and daughters Marilyn Runkel Hemstad and Prasannata (Karen) Runkel fondly remembered not only their father's conservation career but also Sylvan's younger days as he began raising a family and entered World War II.

Sons Tom, Jon, and Jeff Runkel recalled their great respect for their father and his love for his family, his joy of living, his dedication to protecting natural communities, and his commitment to education.

Cindy Howell, a patient friend and skillful editor, helped to polish the rough edges of our writing. Sylvan's granddaughter Karisa Runkel used her graphic design talents to assemble our collection of manuscripts and photos into what we hope is an attractive, coherent publication.

Most of all, we're indebted to the countless people whose lives Sylvan touched through his books, workshops, television programs, Scouting activities, and dedication to conservation causes. Through their own connection to the Earth, all of these "fellow citizens" will assure that Sylvan's spirit lives on.

FOREWORD

A Tribute to Sylvan Runkel — By Dean M. Roosa

"These natural communities have been solving their problems of over-population, waste disposal, and disease for centuries. Perhaps we should take a lesson from them," he told a group of teachers at the State 4-H Camp at Luther as he stood with a twinkle in his eyes and wearing a hat he acquired in 1933.

This was the first time I saw Sylvan "Sy" Runkel, and he was doing what he did best — interpreting a woodland to a group of teachers. That was a long time ago. I saw him many times afterward, and each time he was dealing in some way with natural communities — interpreting them, trying to save them, planning for management of them, looking for rare plants in them, or just enjoying them. He was the closest thing Iowa had to a "living legend" in the natural history field.

He began his work in interpretive science with schools, long before it was a popular field; indeed, before the science had a name. He continued his activity until the end of his life. He was "booked up" each spring season with outdoor classrooms and teacher seminars.

Many people were first introduced to woodlands by taking a walk with Sylvan, listening to him describe the community before them as a living entity, something akin to an organism, complete with all the systems that keep an organism going. It was impossible to ever again look at a woodland in the same way after the gentle and loving presentation that was unique to Sy.

Sy "retired" in 1972; however, it would be more accurate to say his career simply took a new direction as he seemed to be busier in retirement than when he was a full-time employee.

For nearly six decades Sy lectured, educated, entertained, cajoled, served on boards, traveled the state, conducted workshops — all in the name of protecting natural communities he so loved. His influence on Iowa, Iowans, and natural areas continued to the end of his life. I am proud to have counted him among my friends.

INTRODUCTION

Like many Iowans, we grew to admire Sylvan Runkel through our occasional encounters with him at teacher workshops or meetings of environmental groups. Those in-person experiences reinforced the impressions we'd formed from seeing his memorable appearances on Iowa Public Television and, of course, from using the wildflower guides he coauthored.

Through his former job as outdoor writer for *The Des Moines Register*, Larry first met Sylvan in 1972 and thereafter called on him often for expert opinions on natural history. Sylvan's enthusiasm and vast knowledge of Iowa's outdoors made him a favorite of other reporters as well.

Jon met Sylvan at Nature Conservancy meetings and recognized his keen insights about Iowa's natural heritage. Jon eagerly accepted Sylvan's casual invitations to visit the naturalist at his home in Des Moines. The two men enjoyed discussing environmental subjects and Jon never tired of hearing Sylvan's stories of his youthful adventures. Both Jon and Larry grew to cherish

Sylvan's friendship, his counsel on conservation issues, his hospitality, and his good humor.

After Sylvan died in 1995, Jon began searching for a way to preserve the unique legacy of the man we considered to be Iowa's foremost naturalist. Larry was easily persuaded to assist in the project, which we naively assumed might take a year or so.

When we decided to tell Sylvan Runkel's story, however, we didn't realize the number of coauthors we'd have! Foremost, Sylvan told the stories himself, primarily in tape recordings done with his son Tom. But many other people — from casual acquaintances to long-time coworkers — also wanted the chance to share anecdotes about their experiences with this delightful man.

We were struck by people's uniformly positive memories of Sylvan and his contributions to conservation. This book reflects not only our respect for Sylvan and his beliefs, but also the fond recollections of others who admired him. If he had faults — and what human being doesn't? — Sylvan's shortcomings were overwhelmed by the genuine affection he earned from his friends.

As we talked to Sylvan's family and friends, browsed through his voluminous stacks of papers, files, and books, and pondered his fascinating life, our simple tribute to Sylvan gradually evolved into a love affair. Besides being a dedicated conservationist, Sylvan was an unforgettable character whose spirit of adventure, good humor, and zest for life touched thousands of people.

For readers who knew Sylvan Runkel, we trust these stories will remind you of pleasant times, or reveal some new facets of an extraordinary human being. For those of you who never had the privilege of knowing Sylvan in person, we hope we've painted a picture that will help you understand why the Runkel legacy remains so strong among Iowa naturalists.

But our fondest wish is that at least some of these stories will bring a smile to your face and motivate you to "have fun" in the outdoors. That may be the greatest tribute to Sylvan T. Runkel.

CHAPTER 1

THE FOUNDATION

BECKY JANE'S FARM – "THAT WAS HIS FOUNDATION."

How does an Illinois youngster grow into Iowa's best-known and most beloved naturalist? From the time of his birth in 1906, Sylvan T. Runkel followed an adventuresome road that seemed to wind through the pages of American history. He visited his grandmother's log cabin, rode freight trains across the West, worked on an ocean steamer, drove a Model T Ford, fought forest fires, struggled through the Great Depression, climbed mountains, flew biplanes and gliders, won a Purple Heart, taught conservation, explored wilderness areas, and raised a loving family.

Sylvan's sister Geneva Runkel Henss painted this picture of the southern Illinois log cabin where she and Sylvan spent summers with their grandmother, Rebecca Jane Pickett Barnett.

What sparked that love of adventure and fascination with the natural world? Was it genetics or environment? Nature or nurture? How much can your ancestry shape your life? A look at his family tree suggests that Sylvan's ancestors might not have been the least surprised to see him became a military hero, woodsman, adventurer, storyteller, and musician — as well as a leader whose compassion touched countless lives.

The Runkel family claims ties to royalty who built Runkel Castle on the Lahn River north of present-day Frankfort, Germany, in the twelfth century. Several Runkel brothers joined the great migration to America and settled with William Penn in Pennsylvania in the early 1600s.

Sylvan's great-great-great-grandfather Sam McDowell served in the Revolutionary War, then commanded Fort Recovery, Ohio, about 1791, during the Indian Wars. Jacob Runkel, Sylvan's great-great-grandfather, also served in the Revolutionary War. Jacob's son Joseph (Sylvan's great-grandfather) fought in the Civil War. He leg was amputated after he was shot near Pittsburg Landing, Tennessee, during the battle of Shiloh in April 1862. He died as his wife was coming with a wagon to carry her husband home. One of Joseph's sons also was killed at about the same time. A younger son, Thomas Jefferson Runkel (Sylvan's grandfather), told the story years later. Half a century after the war, Sylvan still could sense his grandfather's grief.

Sylvan's maternal grandfather, Felix Barnett, joined the 18th regiment, Illinois Volunteer Infantry, Co. D., in 1861, when he was 21 years old. He served until the end of the Civil War — somehow finding time to court and marry Rebecca Jane "Becky Jane" Pickett in 1863. After the war the couple built a log cabin and settled in Moore's Prairie Township in Jefferson County, Illinois, about 14 miles from Mount Vernon, near the village of Spring Garden. Felix's parents had homesteaded there in the 1840s, while Becky Jane's family had come from Kentucky in a covered wagon. Becky Jane's great-great-grandmother was a Cherokee Indian from Tennessee. Sylvan was proud of his Native American blood.

In the late 1800s southern Illinois retained some of its lawless frontier flavor. Felix Barnett's father, Williamson Barnett, was killed in an argument over a poker game in the 1870s. The Texan he accused of cheating drew a pistol and shot him before Barnett could raise his muzzle-loading rifle to defend himself. Felix kept his father's rifle, which he continued to use for hunting for many years. The Runkel family still prizes the weathered old muzzle-loader, which Sylvan retrieved from the farmstead after Becky Jane died. Sylvan and two cousins walked 14 miles from Mount Vernon to his grandparents' cabin, slept overnight in an outbuilding, then lugged the 18-pound gun back to town. "It's a good, big piece of the history of this country," Sylvan declared later.

Felix Barnett farmed the 40-acre homestead for more than 30 years, growing corn, sorghum, and other crops. His daughter Myrtle (Sylvan's mother) told of following her father's mule-drawn plow and planting kernels of corn in the freshly turned earth. When Felix died in 1897, his widow, Becky Jane, stayed on the southern

Sylvan's maternal grandmother, Rebecca Jane Pickett Barnett, or "Becky Jane," taught Sylvan to love the outdoors.

Illinois farm to scratch out a living for herself and three daughters, including Myrtle. Four other Barnett children already had left home.

Becky Jane survived on hard work and a meager $8 per month government pension Felix had earned as a Civil War veteran. She raised chickens, which ran loose in the farmyard and around the house, and kept a few hogs and cattle. Along with staples such as potatoes, beans, and onions, Becky Jane's huge garden yielded persimmons and "the best rhubarb in the community," declared her granddaughter, Geneva Runkel Henss, who was Sylvan's sister. The family ate most of the produce, but they sold castor beans as a cash crop.

Becky Jane harvested wild bounty as well. She occasionally shot squirrels, rabbits, and other game, and collected berries, poke greens, mushrooms, and roots from the forest. She often used medicinal plants and sometimes helped to deliver babies born on nearby farms.

The children were expected to do their share. Both boys and girls helped with planting. The boys also trapped raccoons, foxes, muskrats, and other animals and sold the fur. With the cash the family could buy a bolt of cloth, and Becky Jane would sew matching shirts and dresses for the youngsters.

Geneva described her grandmother as a true pioneer. Becky Jane cooked on a woodstove and cooled eggs and milk by lowering them into a well in a copper bucket. The family slept on mattresses stuffed with corn shucks and used pillows made with the down of geese they raised. Becky

Jane also spun wool into yarn, which she colored with dye made from walnut hulls and other natural materials. She wove or knitted mittens, blankets, and socks. Once a week Becky Jane built a fire under a huge kettle to heat water for washing clothes.

If she needed to go somewhere — which she seldom did — Becky Jane hitched up the horse and buggy. Although motor vehicles were becoming more common, occasional visitors tied their horses to a hitching rail in front of the log cabin.

When he was only about 4 years old, Sylvan began spending summers with Becky Jane. Geneva remembers Sylvan's keen interest and insatiable curiosity in his grandmother's activities. He followed her around the farmyard and the forest as she shared her woods lore. Sylvan quickly came to feel at home in the outdoors, and he yearned to explore wild places.

Sylvan's sister Geneva Runkel Henss still treasures the mandolin that her father played to court her mother before the couple married in 1903.

Sylvan and two cousins relished the farm life as only three young boys could. They built a small log cabin, caught turtles, frogs, and snakes, and tried to ride the calves. Once, when they impulsively went skinny-dipping in the creek, they got a switching that hurt even more than the sunburn they'd suffered. Sylvan's younger sisters, Geneva and Dorothy, also summered at Becky Jane's, where they could run barefoot along the dusty road and savor the pink clumps of wild roses that grew in the ditches.

When the children visited their grandmother, they slept either on the floor of her cabin or in a loft. The front door often stood open to let in the cool night air. Nobody seemed to mind the bugs. "It was the way things were," said Sylvan, when recalling his happy days there.

Becky Jane also taught the youths to respect their "fellow citizens," as Sylvan later called wild plants and animals. When Sylvan and his cousins captured three baby opossums and proudly brought them to the farmstead, their grandmother ordered the boys to return the animals to their home in the woods.

For about 10 summers Sylvan looked forward to the visits with Becky Jane, her patient explanations of the plants that she knew and used, and the freedom to roam the woods, wetlands, and streams near her cabin. He developed a love of trees and flowers and a fascination with the mysteries of the natural world. "That was his foundation," Geneva declared. Becky Jane's work ethic and spunk made an enduring impression on her grandson, as well.

Sylvan also may have admired the courage and mettle of his Aunt Mime, who lived in a tidy little cabin along Log Cabin Lane not far from Becky Jane's farm. Mime, a sister of Sylvan's mother, had lost her sight as a child, but she shrugged off the adversity. When Mime wanted to visit the rest of the family, she walked fearlessly along the dirt road, yodeling for help if she lost her way.

A generation before, these self-reliant country folk also had caught the attention of another free spirit, Cleveland Arthur Runkel, who came from Madison, Illinois, to court Myrtle. Cleveland would ride the train to a station a few miles from the farm, hire a horse and buggy, then drive down the dusty road singing and playing a mandolin as he approached the Barnett cabin. Decades later, Geneva sighed as she imagined her mother caught in the charms of the dashing young man. Myrtle eloped with Cleveland on August 14, 1903.

The young couple settled in Jacksonville, Illinois, where their first child, Sylvan Thomas Runkel, was born. They later moved to Mount Vernon, then to Moline, where Sylvan spent most of his boyhood.

Becky Jane stayed on the farm until 1920, when she was 73. Although her children finally persuaded her to move to an easier life in Mount Vernon, the loss of her freedom may have broken her spirit. Sylvan's beloved grandmother died several months later.

On the bitter-cold day of the funeral, Sylvan and Geneva kept warm by running alongside the sleigh that carried Becky Jane's casket to the cemetery at Ham's Grove Missionary Baptist Church, just up the road from her cabin. Sylvan never forgot how the mourners sobbed as their matriarch was laid to rest in a plot beside her husband. Years later, Sylvan recalled the sound of the chunks of dirt thumping on the casket, as farmers from the neighborhood shoveled the clay soil back into the grave. "It was like doomsday to hear that," he said.

But Becky Jane's independence lived on in her children. Myrtle, Sylvan's mother, who lived to be 94, loved to tell stories of her girlhood on the farm. Becky Jane's son William Stanifer also clung to the pioneer life and for a time lived in a log cabin on the home place. Later, "Uncle Stan," as Sylvan called him, moved to the boot heel of Missouri. Sylvan made several trips to visit Uncle Stan, where he hunted, fished, and explored the intriguing cypress swamp country.

With this colorful ancestry, perhaps it's no surprise that Sylvan become an independent, self-assured, strong-willed individual. When destiny placed him among the rich natural wonders of the Mississippi River Valley, his life as a respected naturalist began to take shape.

CHAPTER 2

THE BUDDING NATURALIST

"I WANT YOU TO BE AS FREE AS A BIRD . . ."

At the time of Sylvan's birth in 1906, the horse and buggy still ruled the mud streets of his hometown of Jacksonville, Illinois. Sylvan recalled trying to walk through the mire and getting stuck so badly that he had to call for a passerby to pull him out. When a "horseless carriage" chanced to drive by, people might run from their homes shouting "Automobile! Automobile!" then gather to watch the curious machine.

Sylvan and sister Geneva Runkel about 1910.

As Sylvan grew the country and the world around him were changing dramatically. He witnessed rapid advances in transportation, industry, agriculture, and communications that transformed the foundations of American society.

When he was about 5 years old, Sylvan marveled at a flight demonstration by none other than Orville and Wilbur Wright. The famed brothers, on tour with their flying machine, got airborne for a few seconds from a pasture on the edge of Jacksonville. Sylvan always remembered that rather unspectacular flight and the crowd's awe at the invention that would revolutionize the world.

Even as a rush of technology was sweeping the country, the Runkels, like many Midwestern families, clung to their rural roots. They tended a

huge garden, growing peas, beans, radishes, potatoes, cucumbers, and onions. When they lived in Jacksonville, the family kept several cows in a small pasture beside their house. Sylvan and his sister Geneva sometimes sold buckets of milk to their neighbors. The children eagerly awaited regular deliveries from the ice man with his horse-drawn wagon. Sometimes there would be an ice cream treat as well.

When Sylvan was 9 years old, the family moved to Moline, Illinois. Sylvan and Geneva and their younger sister, Dorothy,

Sylvan and sister Geneva Runkel approximately 1910.

who was called "Dorf," liked the excitement of the industrial city, but they looked forward to summer visits to their grandmother's pioneer farm in the backwoods of southern Illinois.

Even in Moline, the Runkel kids grew up close to nature. Their modest home on 48th Street sat within half a block of rugged, undeveloped, wooded Mississippi River bluffs. "We thought it was our own private woods," Geneva recalled. "That was our playground." As he later taught others to do, Sylvan also got acquainted with a host of inhabitants of the forest. "All the little wildflowers were his friends," said Geneva. "He knew them all."

The Mississippi River, as yet untamed by locks and dams, flowed just three blocks from their door. The legendary river was home to steamboats, a procession of commercial fishermen and clammers, clouds of waterfowl, and secret swimming holes. Cleveland and Myrtle Runkel encouraged their children to explore the Mississippi and the nearby Rock River, and to roam the adjoining hills.

"Dad said, 'I want you to be as free as a bird,'" recalled Geneva. "He gave us free rein. He said, 'Do as you like, but never do anything that you wouldn't do if I were standing there.'" So the three Runkel kids, with their parents' blessings, enjoyed all kinds of high adventures. They climbed trees and bluffs and swam and boated on the rivers. Sylvan built his own stilts, then strutted around the Runkel yard. He practiced archery with bows and arrows he'd made. Sylvan and Geneva learned tightrope-walking on a rope that Cleveland had secured between two trees.

"We made our own entertainment," Geneva said. She and Sylvan enlarged a groundhog den to make a cave in the bluff, where they often played, camped, and even cooked meals of frogs' legs. A stray chicken once became a dinner "guest." Dorf and the neighborhood kids sometimes joined the excitement. On summer nights the Runkel children frequently slept out under the stars on a porch roof.

In winter the Runkel kids and their friends zoomed down snow-covered hills on a homemade toboggan, or on crude skis made from barrel staves. They ice-skated on frozen backwaters of the nearby Mississippi.

"We did all those yummy things," Geneva said, reminiscing about her delightful childhood. "Every episode was an adventure," she laughed. "We were allowed to, and we just did it!"

Along with his keen interest in nature, Sylvan cultivated a fascination with motorcycles. Cleveland tinkered with several cycles and occasionally gave his children rides. Sylvan especially looked forward to outings when he and his dad could ride a motorcycle to their favorite rabbit-hunting sites.

The rest of the family also loved the outdoors. They'd often pack a lunch — fried chicken was the family favorite — then ride the streetcar to the ferry landing, where they would catch an excursion boat to a park on Campbell's Island. Occasionally the Runkels would row their own boat to a secluded spot on a bank of the Mississippi.

That's not to say that the youngsters always behaved perfectly, or that they never faced any perils. For example, Sylvan carried a lifelong scar on his face after he cut himself during horseplay with a Civil War sword.

Geneva nearly drowned one summer afternoon when she and Sylvan and some companions were swimming in the Hennepin Canal along the Rock River. The

Sylvan as a toddler.

kids found a rope dangling from a bridge and began swinging over the water and jumping in. When Geneva swung, the rope broke and dropped with her into the canal. Tangled in the line, she barely managed to struggle

Sylvan and his sister Geneva climbed aboard a photographer's mule for this picture about 1912.

to the surface and scream for help. Some of the boys thought she was joking. But Sylvan, who was about 15 years old, immediately jumped in, freed her from the rope, and pulled his frightened sister to safety.

On another occasion Sylvan rescued Dorf while the siblings were swimming in the Mississippi. When his little sister grew too tired to continue, she put her hands on Sylvan's shoulders and he towed her to shore. Geneva also recalled a sudden storm catching the Runkel kids and their father by surprise as they fished on the Mississippi. As waves crashed over the gunnels, they used tin cans to bail the boat until they reached the shore.

Sylvan sometimes even created his own challenges. After several acquaintances drowned when their boat capsized in rapids on the Mississippi near their home, Sylvan vowed to master the river. He built his own boat — and successfully navigated the white water. "We were adventuresome," Geneva chuckled. "And we did a lot of living on the river!"

Sylvan read and re-read Mark Twain's classics *Tom Sawyer* and *The Adventures of Huckleberry Finn*, no doubt comparing the fictional youngsters' exploits with his own. He especially liked Huck's tales of rafting on the Mississippi.

To Sylvan, the lure of the Mississippi was irresistible. Geneva tells of her brother swimming back from the far side of the river carrying a snake he'd caught. He found plenty of excuses to explore the riverbanks and to hang out with local "river rats." Occasionally, he'd persuade steamboat captains to give him a ride, or to allow him into the pilothouse to briefly take the wheel of the big boats.

During junior high and high school Sylvan sometimes walked to the river, rowed three miles downstream to Sixteenth Street, then walked nine blocks up the hill to school. In the afternoon, he would walk down to the river, then row upstream and home.

One of his fondest boyhood memories was of shooting his first duck on the Mississippi in 1920, when he was 14. Federal laws had ended the market hunting and spring shooting of the 1800s, but older hunters still told incredible tales of the clouds of waterfowl that once had swarmed over the river.

The freedom that Sylvan's parents granted to their son created learning opportunities. Sylvan developed respect for the river and the powers of nature. His curiosity about wild things and untamed places nurtured a sense of wonder that he never outgrew.

That interest in nature also was fueled by an amiable man named Rudy Bracker, who started Moline's first Boy Scout troop. Sylvan joined the troop, thrived on the camping trips and other outdoor activities, and earned his First Class badge. In summer the Scouts attended Camp Mansur, just east of Moline, where the boys practiced woodcraft skills. When he turned 18 — too old to be a regular Scout — Sylvan stayed with the troop as an assistant leader. But one Scout outing ended tragically when a youth contracted typhoid fever

Myrtle Runkel with her son, Sylvan, and daughters Dorothy and Geneva about 1915.

and died after drinking from a polluted stream. Sylvan had tried to warn his thirsty companion, but the boy would not listen. Their friend's needless death haunted Sylvan and the other young Scouts.

As he reached adolescence Sylvan welcomed urban adventures along with his rural experiences. He relished the excitement of the Quad Cities metropolitan area, which was a center of commerce, railroads, and factories. Trolleys and Model Ts sped along the streets. Sylvan and his chums sometimes swung from the trolley wires. (When he recalled the reckless behavior decades later, he insisted that he'd been very careful to avoid getting electrocuted.) Like many other young boys, he earned spending money with a paper route delivering the *Moline Dispatch*.

Cleveland and Myrtle Runkel encouraged their children to partake of urban cultural opportunities as well. Sylvan learned ballroom dancing and took a china-painting class. When his mother suggested a year of piano lessons, Sylvan agreed and obediently practiced two hours per day.

Sylvan impressed his family with his musical talent. On Saturday afternoons, after listening to the live piano player at the silent movies in Moline's LeClaire Theater, Sylvan would come home and play by ear the tunes he'd just heard. Sometimes he'd visit a music store to hear a pianist play requests from customers. Later he would sit down at the Runkel piano and pick out the same melodies. His gift for song and the piano became a lifelong passion. "He could make a piano walk around the room," boasted his sister Geneva. "He could just make it ring."

The gift for music may have run in the family. Cleveland Runkel loved to sing, and he played guitar, mandolin, accordion, piano, and mouth organ. Sylvan's sister Dorothy also was an accomplished pianist. As a girl, she sang on a Quad Cities radio station.

Geneva remembers Sylvan as a gregarious youth to whom his peers often turned for guidance. When he and Geneva and their Christian Endeavor group were asked to help teach vacation Bible school at the Union Congregational Church in Moline, Sylvan instinctively took his class into the woods to get in touch with the wonders of creation.

On another occasion the patriotic Runkel children held a solemn funeral for a worn-out American flag. They made a small coffin, held a ceremony, and respectfully buried the red, white, and blue banner.

A more spontaneous celebration — Armistice Day, November 11, 1918 — etched the significance of world events into Sylvan's young mind. With the end of the brutal World War, people around the globe poured into the streets to rejoice at the signing of the truce.

Moline was no different. When 12-year-old Sylvan heard of the jubilation, he tried to ride a trolley downtown to join the festivities, but the press of the crowd forced the streetcar to stop. Everyone, including the trolley operator, got off to cheer and shout as they paraded along the streets. The wide-eyed youth was swept up in a history lesson more powerful than any he could have learned in a classroom.

Cleveland and Myrtle encouraged that kind of interest in national and world affairs. They sometimes assigned their children to study the encyclopedia, take notes, and introduce a discussion topic at the dinner table.

"We'd bring up something and Sylvan and I would both talk about it," Geneva said. "And that would bring in the rest of the family." Instead of gossiping about the neighbors, the Runkels engaged in intellectual conversations. "That really broadened our scope," Geneva said. "It stretched our minds."

To expand her children's horizons even more, Myrtle planned a trip to the mountains of Colorado in 1920, when Sylvan was 13, Geneva 11, and Dorothy 6. At the time, Cleveland worked for the railroad, so the family traveled at discount rates. To raise spending money for the excursion, Sylvan and his sisters tended an even larger garden than usual and sold the produce to neighbors.

The vacationers went to Pike's Peak, where they rode to the top in a taxi.

Cleveland and Myrtle Runkel with their son, Sylvan, and daughters Dorothy (center) and Geneva about 1917.

They visited other tourist attractions, such as Garden of the Gods, the Cave of the Winds, Seven Falls, Manitou Springs, and Green Mountain Springs. Sylvan loved the adventure and often scrambled to the highest overlooks as Myrtle fretted over his safety. The trip may have whetted his appetite for the American West.

For Sylvan a highlight of that summer was his climb up Cheyenne Peak, near Colorado Springs, to the isolated grave of Helen Hunt Jackson, a writer and poet who had championed the cause of Native Americans. As a teenager, Sylvan already had developed an interest in the plight of

Sylvan and sisters Geneva and Dorf Runkel riding a cart pulled by a goat, approximately 1918.

native peoples and their land, as well as a quiet pride in the Cherokee heritage of his great-grandmother, Marget Ann Hackworth. For the rest of his life, Sylvan cherished a small stone that he brought back from the mountain where Jackson was buried.

Part of Sylvan's fascination with Native Americans may have grown from visits to Black Hawk Park near Moline for annual Labor Day weekend powwows. He and Geneva would hike about six miles to the park to see the teepees, dancing, cooking demonstrations, and colorful costumes.

On quieter Sunday afternoons neighbors gathered to make popcorn, ice cream, or taffy. "We would usually sit around and listen to the old folks talk," Sylvan wrote later. "I always thought it was just about the most interesting thing there was — to listen to the conversations and stories of the older folks."

Sometimes friends and family gathered around the kitchen table to try to pick out voices coming from the primitive crystal set Cleveland had built. They marveled at the miracle called "radio."

Sylvan and Geneva also polished their speaking skills at an early age. On summer nights in those days before television, air-conditioning, and shopping malls, the Runkel children sometimes sat on their porch and told stories to other young friends.

The mental gymnastics were second nature to both Cleveland and Myrtle. When she was a girl, Myrtle's parents had challenged her and her siblings by holding "ciphering" (math) contests. The youngsters wrote on slates by the light of kerosene lamps while sitting around the fireplace in their log cabin. Myrtle excelled in school, where she was the perennial spelling bee champion, and later was certified to teach. Her father discouraged her from taking a teaching job, however. Felix did not want his teenage daughter to face the rigors of teaching in a remote country school, where she would have had to ride horseback and arrive early on winter mornings to build a fire.

Cleveland "was really a brain," Geneva declared. Although he only completed the eighth grade, he was an expert machinist and became a foreman at the Yellow Sleeve Valve Engine Works in East Moline. He received several awards for developing innovations to make the plant's machinery more efficient. What's more, Geneva asserted, her clever father even had worked out the principles of airplane flight independently of two other young inventors named Orville and Wilbur Wright.

Despite his lack of a high school education, Cleveland also wrote poetry and often helped Sylvan and Geneva with their homework. Before Sylvan enrolled at Iowa State College in Ames, Cleveland hired a tutor to help his son sharpen his math skills and better prepare him for higher education.

Cleveland and Myrtle insisted that Sylvan take Latin in high school, assuring him that he would need the language for his future studies in medical school. Sylvan eventually persuaded his family that he did not want to be a doctor, and sometimes joked that his name almost required that he become a forester. But Latin training served him well years later when he worked with the scientific names of plants.

Sylvan, Geneva (seated) and Dorothy Runkel, about 1928.

"A jolly and true happy fellow," read the caption under Sylvan's photo in the 1924 Moline High School annual. "Syl," as his classmates called him, was an avid reader, a member of the extemporaneous debate team, and a distance runner on the track team. He landed a role in the school musical, "Top 'O the Mornin.'"

Sylvan had developed an itch to see the world as well. He and some high school pals occasionally set off on camping trips, when they hitchhiked wherever their whims would lead and slept where darkness found them. After they awoke one night in a thunderstorm to see cemetery gravestones illuminated by lightning, they became a little more careful about their choice of beds.

One excursion led as far as Nebraska, with a stop in Iowa to sleep under a bridge over the Des Moines River. "We got a ride with some people that were going to Omaha, so thought we would go along," Sylvan nonchalantly wrote home on a postcard. "Will be back as soon as I can make it. Sylvan."

Sylvan's youthful curiosity and excitement about the natural world laid the foundation for even more adventures as an adult. He could not contain his infectious enthusiasm for life and for exploring the marvels of our planet.

"He was just an older kid," said Dean Roosa, who knew him best after Sylvan had reached retirement age. "He never lost his child-like joy of living." The men worked closely together on the State Preserves Advisory Board and to write two wildflower books.

The late John Madson, in the dedication to his book *The Tallgrass Prairie*, may have paid Sylvan the ultimate tribute: "To Sy Runkel and his ageless, unfailing sense of wonder."

CHAPTER 3

OUT WEST

"I HAD A SORT OF ACHING TO SEE WHAT WAS OUT IN THE WEST . . ."

Like many of his classmates, Sylvan got a job soon after he graduated from Moline High School in the spring of 1924. He worked as a clerk in Fiske and Loosley's grocery store in downtown Moline, where he managed the fish department and carried 100-pound bags of sugar and flour for customers.

Unlike some of his friends, Sylvan had no intention of settling down for a life in a traditional retail, farm, or factory job. After a year as a grocery boy, he longed for adventure. "I had a sort of aching to see what was out in the west part of the country," Sylvan explained as he recalled the experience years later. "And Mer Buhle [a close friend] was of the same idea. So we

With his white shirt, coat, tie, and slicked-back hair, Sylvan didn't look much different from his fellow students in the Moline High School class of 1924 — but he already had developed a wanderlust that became lifelong.

thought we'd hitchhike and ride freight trains — however we could get out there — and see what was out there in the West in Montana, and Idaho, and California and those other states."

Fueled with anticipation, $40 in his pocket, and a pack on his back, Sylvan hitchhiked out of Moline with Mer on July 5, 1925. Each carried a sleeping bag improvised from canvas and blankets. They packed oatmeal, sugar, and condensed milk but hoped to earn most meals by washing dishes or doing odd jobs. If they ever needed a shower, they figured, they might find a YMCA.

Sylvan was testing his wings. His parents had encouraged his independence, and wanderlust now lured him away from Moline. Myrtle worried over her son's plans, yet she and Cleveland realized they could not dissuade him. "The world was out there, and we knew he had to go," his sister Geneva explained later.

To ease his mother's anxiety, Sylvan promised to keep in touch. He accepted a stack of postcards and regularly wrote home to tell of his latest escapades — or at least some of them. (The family still treasures those postcards.) We can only guess what exciting details Sylvan left out to spare his mother's nerves. Even with the periodic communications, Sylvan's family knew comparatively little about the trip until he returned home. "We just knew he was out there," Geneva said.

On the first day the eager travelers got as far as Cedar Falls, Iowa, where they spent the night with "great gobs of mosquitos" at a tourist camp. As they continued north into Minnesota the mosquitoes got even worse, Sylvan lamented in a postcard from Northfield.

After traveling 160 miles in one day to reach Duluth, Sylvan confidently predicted that he and Mer could be in California in two weeks. That proved to be a bit optimistic: They didn't arrive until August 13 or 14, more than five weeks later. The boys always had good excuses for their delays. At Virginia, Minnesota, for example, they ended up in jail. Sylvan later joked about the friendly policemen who offered the boys a free bed in the city's brand-new jail. They accepted the honor of being the first "prisoners," although the officers didn't lock the door. (Years later, Sylvan's young son Tom embarrassed his family on a crowded tour bus when he loudly blurted, "Tell me about when Dad was in jail.")

Sylvan and Mer lingered in the "wild and woolly" country of northern Minnesota. "Everything is burnt and cut-over timber. Few farms," Sylvan observed in a postcard. "Swam across the Mississippi River 6 times yesterday afternoon," he wrote home from Bemidji. "It is about 50 feet wide here." Intrigued by the Mississippi River, the boys went 60 miles out of their way, including 23 miles on foot, to see the river's source at Lake Itasca.

Following the old Roosevelt Highway, which in some places was little more than "a couple of ruts," the companions continued west across North Dakota. They sometimes slept in deserted barns or haymows, but realized they were seeing fewer and fewer farms as the woodlands gave way to prairie. With very few cars or people on the road, the boys began hopping freight trains. While riding on open cars, they sometimes amused themselves by tossing rocks at prairie dogs. (The animals had little to fear: The speeding train threw the boys' aim way off the mark.) With broad skies, relentless winds, rolling grasslands, wheat fields, and prairie potholes swarming with waterfowl, the Great Plains of North Dakota seemed wild and untamed to the youths from an Illinois river town.

"We rode all day on that flatcar. It was really nice riding," Sylvan remembered. "You had the whole country open on all sides." Indeed, the young hobos would learn a great deal about riding trains before the trip was over. They sometimes rode on top of boxcars and found themselves dodging wires atop an electric train as it zipped through mountain tunnels. "If we'd have touched that, it would have been the end of the journey," Sylvan mused decades later.

Near Great Falls, Montana, they survived a train wreck while

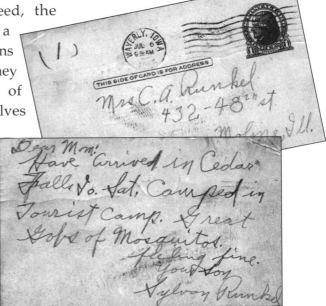

Sylvan's first postcard, written in Cedar Falls, Iowa.

riding on a car loaded with lumber. The train derailed and the car skidded to a halt, slamming the lumber forward against the next train car. Luckily, the boys had decided to ride on the rear of the lumber car, so they escaped unhurt.

Mer Buhle, Sylvan's high school friend and companion on his 1925 trip to explore the West.

Sylvan later chuckled about things he'd learned while riding the rails. Once, he and Mer hopped into a boxcar crowded with transients. The boys were surprised to see a vacant spot to the rear of the open door, but, to their disgust, they soon discovered why the place had not been taken. The hobos made a habit of urinating out the door of the train. Anyone downwind could expect to get sprayed.

On July 15 the boys knew they had reached the real West. "I arrived in Fort Union, Mont., this morning. About 8 different tribes of Indians are holding a big Pow Wow," Sylvan wrote from Bainville, at the confluence of the Missouri and Yellowstone rivers. "The only water in Fort Union to drink must be dipped up from the Missouri River." The parched plains brought one benefit: a respite from the mosquitoes that had plagued the boys for much of the trip.

Sylvan could scarcely contain his excitement about the West. He marveled about the beauty of the Bear Paw Mountains, joked about "lots of Indians, Cowboys, and ranchers running loose," and eagerly anticipated a visit to Glacier National Park.

At Glacier Park Lodge, Sylvan and Mer gawked at huge timbers used in the building's construction. The wanderers had no money to rent a room in the plush hotel, so they camped on nearby Squaw Mountain. They started up the peak but soon ran out of energy. The youths' enthusiasm could not prepare them for the effects of the high elevation. They cooked oatmeal, rolled out their sleeping bags, then slept all night and much of the next day. "We were awfully sleepy," Sylvan said — but not too sleepy to notice a mountain lion on a hill above them.

Still exhausted on the second morning, the boys gave up the climb without reaching the peak. "We figured we'd better get the heck out of there!" Sylvan remembered. Only later did they realize that the thin air had caused their lethargy and labored breathing.

Back on the dusty road, Sylvan and Mer caught a ride in the back of a pickup truck, but they soon went back to walking when the truck stalled on a hill. The driver was too drunk to shift gears.

When the boys reached Yellowstone National Park, they spent almost a week visiting tourists' favorite spots: Morning Glory Spring, Great Falls, Lookout Point, Eagle Nest Rock, Gardiner Canyon, Obsidian Cliff, Fishing Bridge, Castle Geyser, Old Faithful, Grand Canyon of the Yellowstone. "I am practicing running," Sylvan joked on one of several picture postcards. "The park is full of bears. They eat anything edible." The hot springs also fascinated him. "Some have sulfur in them. Smells like dead horse," he wrote.

After making a complete circle of Yellowstone's main attractions, the boys hitchhiked through Idaho, headed for Salt Lake City. By chance, they caught a ride part way with a friend from Moline whom they had encountered at Yellowstone.

In Salt Lake City, Sylvan and Mer marveled at the Great Salt Lake and were inspired by the organist at the Mormon Tabernacle. They feasted at a soup kitchen for transients. "We both filled up for supper," Sylvan noted on a postcard. "A whole supper can be got for 20 cents." Even bean soup probably tasted good after a month on the road!

Sylvan's postcard also asked his sister Geneva to arrange for his high school transcript to be sent to Iowa State College. He intended to head home in time to start forestry classes in the fall.

Sylvan and Mer hoped to go to Los Angeles from Salt Lake City, but the hitchhikers found few prospects for rides across the desert. They hopped aboard a passenger train, where a brakeman quickly confronted the freeloaders and ordered them off.

When a freight train passed, they tried again. A railroad cop quashed that plan when he brandished his big six-shooter and ordered them to stop. The officer threatened to force them to work on a road crew for 30 days, but released them on their promise not to catch any more trains. They went back to hitchhiking. The travelers learned the hard way that some railroads — the Milwaukee and the Northern Pacific, for example — had few rules against people catching rides on trains, while others, such as the Union Pacific, dealt harshly with hobos and hangers-on.

Hitchhiking didn't go much better. Discouraged by the lack of rides, the boys concluded that one person alone might have better luck than two together. So they split up on the edge of Las Vegas, planning to meet at the YMCA in Los Angeles.

Sylvan soon discovered that thumbing his way across the desert was

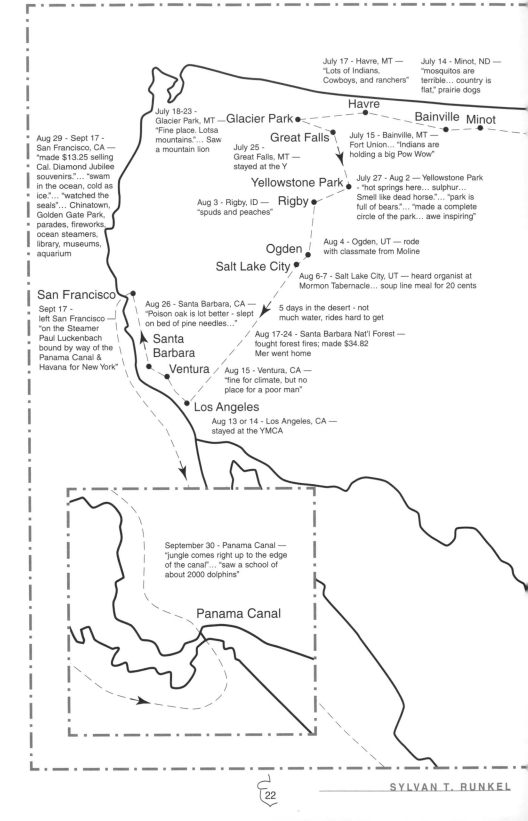

July 17 - Havre, MT — "Lots of Indians, Cowboys, and ranchers"

July 14 - Minot, ND — "mosquitos are terrible… country is flat," prairie dogs

Havre

Bainville   Minot

July 18-23 - Glacier Park, MT — "Fine place. Lotsa mountains."… Saw a mountain lion

Glacier Park

Great Falls

July 15 - Bainville, MT — Fort Union… "Indians are holding a big Pow Wow"

Aug 29 - Sept 17 - San Francisco, CA — "made $13.25 selling Cal. Diamond Jubilee souvenirs."… "swam in the ocean, cold as ice."… "watched the seals"… Chinatown, Golden Gate Park, parades, fireworks, ocean steamers, library, museums, aquarium

July 25 - Great Falls, MT — stayed at the Y

Yellowstone Park

July 27 - Aug 2 — Yellowstone Park - "hot springs here… sulphur… Smell like dead horse."… "park is full of bears."… "made a complete circle of the park… awe inspiring"

Aug 3 - Rigby, ID — "spuds and peaches"

Rigby

Aug 4 - Ogden, UT — rode with classmate from Moline

Ogden

Salt Lake City

Aug 6-7 - Salt Lake City, UT — heard organist at Mormon Tabernacle… soup line meal for 20 cents

San Francisco

Sept 17 - left San Francisco "on the Steamer Paul Luckenbach bound by way of the Panama Canal & Havana for New York"

Aug 26 - Santa Barbara, CA — "Poison oak is lot better - slept on bed of pine needles…"

5 days in the desert - not much water, rides hard to get

Aug 17-24 - Santa Barbara Nat'l Forest — fought forest fires; made $34.82 Mer went home

Santa Barbara

Ventura

Aug 15 - Ventura, CA — "fine for climate, but no place for a poor man"

Los Angeles

Aug 13 or 14 - Los Angeles, CA — stayed at the YMCA

September 30 - Panama Canal — "jungle comes right up to the edge of the canal"… "saw a school of about 2000 dolphins"

Panama Canal

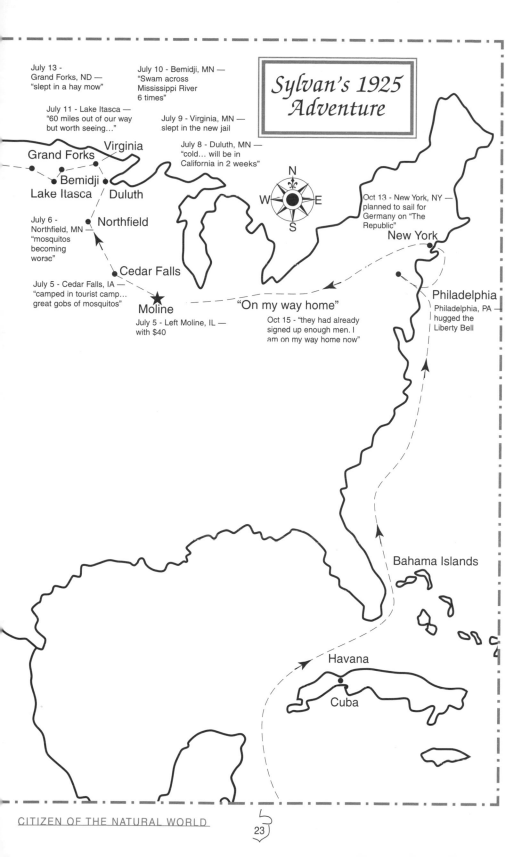

Sylvan's 1925 Adventure

July 13 - Grand Forks, ND — "slept in a hay mow"

July 10 - Bemidji, MN — "Swam across Mississippi River 6 times"

July 11 - Lake Itasca — "60 miles out of our way but worth seeing…"

July 9 - Virginia, MN — slept in the new jail

July 8 - Duluth, MN — "cold… will be in California in 2 weeks"

Oct 13 - New York, NY — planned to sail for Germany on "The Republic"

Virginia

Grand Forks

Bemidji

Lake Itasca / Duluth

July 6 - Northfield, MN — "mosquitos becoming worse"

Northfield

New York

Cedar Falls

July 5 - Cedar Falls, IA — "camped in tourist camp… great gobs of mosquitos"

Moline

July 5 - Left Moline, IL — with $40

"On my way home"

Oct 15 - "they had already signed up enough men. I am on my way home now"

Philadelphia

Philadelphia, PA — hugged the Liberty Bell

Bahama Islands

Havana

Cuba

no easy matter. A rancher gave him a ride, only to drop him at a fork in the road 20 miles from nowhere. "I was very much alone out there on the desert," Sylvan remembered. Fortunately, he had filled his pack with grapes from a field at the edge of Las Vegas. Unfortunately, he got sick from eating "half a peck" of the tasty snacks. He spent a long, cold, miserable night alone on the desert.

The next morning the heat took over. Sylvan started walking and found only an occasional large rock for a little shade. He drank the last of his water. The sun grew hotter. "I was getting a little thirsty," he admitted, when retelling the story later. Finally he came to a cluster of houses, with a water pump in the middle of the tiny village. "I drank too much water," he recalled with a groan. He vowed to treat the desert with more respect.

When a former prospector offered to let him wait at his filling station for a ride, Sylvan readily accepted the offer, not wanting to risk more solitary days or nights in the desert.

Traffic was sparse, but eventually a big car with half a dozen passengers stopped at the station. The other men gruffly persuaded the reluctant driver to take Sylvan to Los Angeles. He was so grateful for the ride that he tried not to think about the risks of riding with the suspicious-looking characters.

Despite his apprehensions about his benefactors, Sylvan made it safely to Los Angeles and met Mer at the YMCA, as planned. The boys visited Hollywood, swam in the ocean, played tourist, and spent Sylvan's last dime on a bucket of oranges. They searched in vain for Sylvan's uncle, Albert Runkel, who might have given them a place to stay or a bit of spending money. Mer apparently grew weary of the travel and the uncertain finances, and he headed back to Moline.

Sylvan refused to give up his adventure, however. On a hunch, he followed the smoke from a forest fire and went to a Santa Barbara National Forest ranger station, seeking a job as firefighter. He was hired on the spot, at a wage of 35 cents an hour. The rangers seldom had such a willing applicant for the fire crews.

Still short of workers, the rangers took a police escort to a local pool hall to seek additional "volunteers." When the rangers came in the front door, the pool players dashed out the back — and into the arms of the waiting cops. Despite their pleas, the men were herded onto a truck and conscripted to work on the fire lines.

Sylvan joined a group of 35 or 40 such ne'er-do-wells, who were ordered to hike into the mountains to the fire site. They started the march at dusk and arrived at 2 a.m., following a narrow, winding trail by lantern light. One hiker slipped off the trail and tumbled down a steep slope into the brush. The rangers rescued the terrified man, who was cut and bruised but not seriously hurt. Once in camp, some of the men began a noisy, all-night dice game, shouting in Spanish over the protests of their companions, who were trying to sleep.

The next day and for the following week Sylvan sweated on a fire line, grubbing out brush to form a firebreak that might keep the flames from spreading through dry chaparral. It was a hot, dirty, backbreaking, dangerous, frustrating job, with work starting at 2 a.m. while the breezes were the calmest. Meals consisted of slumgullion stew. Rattlesnakes sometimes lurked under shrubs. Just when the firefighters thought they might have the blaze contained, gusts of wind could pick up hot sparks and blow them across the line to start new fires.

At one point as the fire approached, an assistant ranger pulled his gun and ordered Sylvan's crew onto a rock pile. "I'll shoot the first son-of-a-bitch that runs," he growled. As the smoke grew thicker and sparks blew onto the men, the would-be hero relented. "Okay, boys, let's get the hell out of here!" he shouted, and the men ran down the valley out of harm's way. The man may have hoped to emulate Edward Pulaski, a ranger who in 1910 had saved his men by herding them into in a mine shaft to escape a wildfire.

Listening to the conversations of his Mexican coworkers, Sylvan tried to learn some Spanish. The Hispanics offered to teach him to say "pass the sugar." But Sylvan couldn't understand why everyone laughed so hard when he repeated "besa mi culo." To his chagrin, he discovered that the phrase really meant "kiss my backside."

The job taught Sylvan a new respect for fires, but he learned one other lesson too late. Noticing a rash on his skin, he realized to his dismay that some of the brush he'd been cutting was, in fact, poison oak. Ironically, the man who was to become an expert botanist had not recognized a common poisonous plant. "I got the dangdest case," he recalled. "I had it all over my legs and arms. I was in kind of a mess."

The chief ranger sent Sylvan back to town to get medical treatment and to pick up his $34.82 paycheck. Since he had not been able to write home for more than a week, Sylvan sent a telegram to his parents as soon as he came off the mountain. "Fought fires one week, was broke, now flush, feel fine, your son." He did not mention the poison oak — and only referred to it briefly in a later postcard.

Although Sylvan finally was getting to see the southern California coast, the next week could hardly be called a dream vacation. Sylvan smeared himself with salve and waited impatiently for the rash and inflammation to subside. He slept in a park near the ocean. "I walked around town and down to the seashore," Sylvan said. "I tried to enjoy myself, but I was kind of miserable with all that poison oak."

He set out for San Francisco, promising his mother in a postcard that he would "start home soon." But Sylvan's curiosity again won out. For more than two weeks he explored the Bay Area. He rode a ferry and wistfully watched ocean steamers in the harbor. He stayed at the YMCA, visited Golden Gate Park, explored Chinatown, browsed through a library and museums, toured the aquarium, watched seals play, and swam in the ocean. While enjoying parades and fireworks that celebrated California's 75th year of statehood, he found that he could earn as much as $13 per day selling medallions honoring the Diamond Jubilee. That pay sure beat fighting fires, he concluded.

On each postcard to his mother he hinted that he would start home soon. But he secretly was longing for a closer look at those magnificent ships out in San Francisco Bay. "I wanted to get on a ship that went to China, and see a little bit more of the world," he said. He tried to get onto the freighters to ask about jobs, but guards on the docks foiled his attempts to reach the boats.

At last, with the help of a friendly policeman, Sylvan landed a job as cook's helper on the steamer *Paul Luckenbach*, which was headed to Philadelphia and New York by way of the Panama Canal. He sent postcards promising to start school in another year, after he had earned more money.

Shortly after the ship left port the boatswain offered him the job of ordinary seaman, or deckhand, which paid $40 per month. This work consisted mostly of scrubbing the deck and painting, but at least Sylvan spent more time up on deck, where he could see the world. That was far better than being cooped up in the galley — and having to explain to fellow sailors why there were cockroaches in the soup.

Sylvan relished the ocean trip. He watched the undulating ocean waves, saw a school of 2,000 dolphins, admired sea birds, breathed fresh sea air, and felt the rise and fall of the ship cutting through the water. He marveled at the Panama Canal, an engineering feat that had been completed only a few years earlier. Although he was supposed to be swabbing the deck, Sylvan often found himself distracted from his work as he studied the tropical vegetation, the canal structure, and the people on shore.

During a stop in Gatun Lake, which is part of the canal, Sylvan and several other sailors decided to swim in the warm, inviting waters. They dove from a rope ladder, splashing alongside the ship. Only later did they learn that they'd shared their swimming hole with crocodiles. "We felt kind of good being out of there," he said afterward.

The ship steamed past Cuba and up the East Coast. The freighter traveled up the Delaware River and

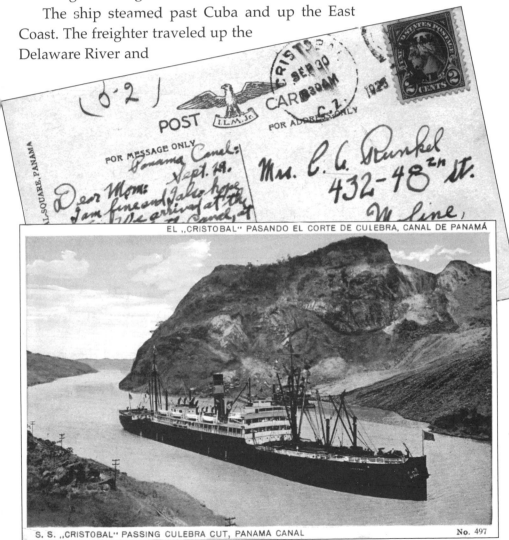

EL „CRISTOBAL" PASANDO EL CORTE DE CULEBRA, CANAL DE PANAMÁ

S. S. „CRISTOBAL" PASSING CULEBRA CUT, PANAMA CANAL   No. 497

Sylvan sent his mother a picture postcard describing the wonders of the Panama Canal.

laid over a couple of days in Philadelphia, where Sylvan went ashore to see Independence Hall. He was deeply moved by the experience. "I gave the Liberty Bell a hug," he confessed decades later. "You weren't supposed to touch it, but I did. So I have touched the bell which rang out freedom for this country."

When the ship reached New York, Sylvan faced a dilemma. He had enjoyed his sea adventure and wanted to continue. He signed on with the *USS Republic*, which was bound for Germany. But he realized that his parents might be worried about him, and that he had planned to go to college. So, on October 13, 1925, he wrote separate postcards to his mother and father:

"Dear Pop: I'm fine and hope you are also. And I have remained and shall remain true to your teachings and wishes. I am shipped on the steamer Republic bound for Germany... As ever, your son — Sylvan."

"Dear Mom: ... Now don't you worry about this a bit for I have $3 and I will not telegraph for money and I shall start college next fall with money I shall earn on a boat sailing to Germany suddenly.... I shall be back in a couple of months. With much love, Sylvan."

Sylvan boarded the *Republic*, preparing for departure. He was assigned a bunk and slept onboard. But when the captain called the roll the next morning, Sylvan's name was not included. The roster had been overbooked; there was no more room for another crewman.

"I was kinda disappointed," he admitted later. Still confident that he could get a job, he headed for the office of the Seaman's Institute, which places sailors on ships. But then he recalled the fatherly advice of the ship captain, who had urged Sylvan to return home and get a college education.

"I got to thinking, I'm supposed to be in forestry school this fall," he reminisced. "And here this was almost November and it was gettin' cold and rainy; by gosh, I think I'll just hitchhike right on back, which is what I did."

He wrote one last card to his mother: "I'm on my way home now."

More than six decades later, Sylvan recalled his quandary as he stood on that pier and pondered whether to take the next boat to Europe or to return to the Midwest and go to college. He sometimes speculated on what his life would have been like if he had chosen more ocean adventures. But instead of heading out to sea he hitchhiked west, heading back to Moline.

In Pittsburgh he stopped at the police station to seek shelter from a cold October rain. The officers showed him to the basement, where he slept on a wooden door laid on the floor. Not until the next morning did he see the cockroach "as big as a mouse" lurking under the makeshift bed.

Sylvan returned safely to Moline but stayed for only a few weeks before leaving again. This trip was much shorter. Needing money for college, he took a job near Hillsdale, Illinois, about 15 miles from Moline, helping a farmer to pick corn by hand. He made five cents a bushel and could pick about 50 bushels per day, tossing the ears into a horse-drawn wagon. He envied the more experienced pickers who sometimes topped 100 bushels per day.

"That pickin' corn was a kinda rough way of workin' and livin'," conceded Sylvan, who'd seen his share of hard work. He slept in an unheated farmhouse bedroom and arose before daylight to hitch up the horses. He walked all day beside the wagon, and sometimes had to scoop off the load of corn as well as pick it. He was glad when Christmas came and he could quit the job and prepare to enroll in forestry classes at Iowa State College.

The experiences of 1925 helped to mold the rest of Sylvan's life. What began with a youth's curiosity about the West turned into a cross-country odyssey. The trip fueled a wanderlust that lured Sylvan again and again to follow his own advice to "get acquainted" with wild places. During breaks from school and on job-hunting trips, he continued to hitchhike and ride freight trains across the country for several years. Even in his later years, he entertained family and friends with stories of adventures — and misadventures — on his 1925 wanderings.

As an Iowa State College student about 1930, Sylvan proudly donned the clothing of a future forester.

SYLVAN T. RUNKEL

CHAPTER 4

FORESTRY SCHOOL

"HE ENJOYED LIFE."

Although Sylvan had intended to begin studying forestry at Iowa State College in the fall of 1925, the excitement of exploring California and the lure of adventures at sea overpowered his immediate desire to start school. Still, his trip had helped him to realize the importance of an education in finding a job, so he vowed that he would come back in time for the winter quarter.

Why Iowa State? Noted conservationist and *Des Moines Register* editorial cartoonist J. N. "Ding" Darling may have influenced Sylvan's decision. Darling launched a strong defense of Iowa State's forestry curriculum in 1925, after the Iowa Board of Education recommended ending the program as an economy move. Darling and executives from *The Register* and *Wallace's Farmer* fought to maintain the forestry curriculum. R. A. Pearson, president of Iowa State, and Charles F. Curtiss, dean of agriculture, also stepped in to help forestry to escape the chopping block.

Thus, Sylvan was able to keep his promise to become an Iowa State forester. In January 1926 he boarded a train from Rock Island to Ames, where he began his college career.

He lost no time in getting into the swing of college living. By the fall of 1926 Sylvan and a number of other carefree foresters had joined Sigma Pi fraternity. Sylvan also sampled college athletics. He wrestled on the intramural squad, tried competitive swimming, pole-vaulted, ran the 100-yard dash, and occasionally did some boxing.

"He was a person who enjoyed life," recalled Sigma Pi fraternity brother Orland Branson. "He always seemed to be in good humor. I never saw him get cross or irritated at anything."

G. B. MacDonald, head of the forestry department at Iowa State College, was Sylvan's favorite professor. (IOWA STATE UNIVERSITY/SPECIAL COLLECTIONS DEPARTMENT)

His love of a good time occasionally got Sylvan into trouble, however. He and another fraternity brother, national champion wrestler Hugh Linn, once were reprimanded for serenading a sorority house. School officials alleged that the boys had sung a bawdy version of "Barnacle Bill the Sailor." Sylvan, Hugh, and the flattered women insisted that the song was "Jesus Wants Me for a Sunbeam."

Along with his college-style amusements, Sylvan did find some time for his studies. He also developed a lifelong friendship with Professor Gilmour B. MacDonald, "Prof Mac," who headed the forestry department and was a leader in the state and national conservation movements. MacDonald was a member of the Iowa Conservation Association and served on an advisory committee that helped to persuade the state legislature to establish a state park system. A strong advocate of private land forestry and a contributor to Iowa's landmark "Twenty-five Year Conservation Plan," MacDonald helped to establish the Iowa State Forest Nursery.

During each summer break, Sylvan went in search of another adventure. In 1926 he traveled to Iowa State's Forestry Summer Camp on Michigan's Upper Peninsula, near Ontonagon, where new students were expected to get "the smell of the woods." Sylvan's nose, and the rest of his senses, liked what he found. The would-be foresters swam in the ice-cold Iron River and explored virgin hemlock stands around the site of today's Porcupine Mountain State Park.

Along with their field trips and timber cruising, the high-spirited youths found ample time for entertainment, which often included Sylvan dancing a jig on a wooden floor improvised from an old barn door. His fellow students teased him about his fancy footwork, and about his propensity to be late for dinner.

Sylvan also went on a field trip with legendary Iowa botanist Dr. Louis Pammel. Years later, that outing stuck in his mind as the way not to introduce people to plants. Pammel, who was in his 80s, simply identified species using their Latin names.

"I followed him around that day, and at the end of the day I had five solid pages of notebook notations just full of scientific names — and I didn't have the foggiest notion of what the plants were," Sylvan laughed. "It took a long time for me to ever figure that out later on." That experience with Pammel may have helped to persuade Sylvan that a wildflower hike should include lively stories — not just be a pedantic taxonomy lecture.

Still, Sylvan probably figured that even a dull field trip was better than classroom work. The footloose youth left his classes at Iowa State in the middle of spring quarter of 1927. He and a friend hitchhiked west after a detour through Saint Louis to see Sylvan's grandfather, Thomas Jefferson Runkel. The travelers passed through the Kansas prairies and within sight of Pike's Peak, Colorado. They browsed the New Mexico Art Museum in Santa Fe and toured Arizona's Petrified Forest. Sylvan claimed in a postcard to have seen cowboy movie star Tom Mix, "driving a big car out on the Ariz. Desert." He toured Los Angeles and went deep-sea fishing with a favorite uncle, Albert Runkel. He sent home picture postcards of orange groves, adobe missions, and movie stars' mansions.

Sylvan then meandered up the Pacific Coast, stopping in northern California to see Mount Lassen, which was billed as the country's only active volcano. "It isn't doing anything that I can tell," he wrote home, clearly disappointed at the lack of fireworks.

His money began to run low, but Sylvan tried to reassure his mother with frequent postcards. "If you were worrying, which I hope you weren't, please refrain because I have this day received a job," he wrote in late April. So what if it was only a job as a "swamper," clearing brush along trails, or a later stint on a road crew? The food was good and Sylvan was outdoors, savoring the mountains and the West.

Before long he got an offer he couldn't refuse. The U. S. Forest Service needed a fire lookout at Windy Camp, a mountain in southwestern Oregon's Umpqua National Forest. Sylvan hiked 12 miles from the Tiller Ranger Station up to the peak and settled in for a summer of isolation. He eagerly scaled a massive Douglas fir tree, which had been cut off near its top to install an observation platform about 70 feet above the ground. From the lookout he could see almost 50 miles to Crater Lake.

Living at the base of the lookout in a windowless, 13-foot-square cabin with a plank for a bed and packrats and deer for neighbors, Sylvan learned the meaning of solitude. He saw only 13 other people during his three-month stay. Several of the visitors were prospectors, who were following rumors in search of a lost gold mine.

Sylvan drew his drinking water from a cold spring and carried it 500 feet up the mountain in a five-gallon can strapped to a packboard. Every couple of weeks a wrangler with a packhorse brought food and other supplies; however, during one 23-day stretch, the packer could not reach the lookout because he was too busy serving firefighting crews. For several days, Sylvan lived on prunes and hardtack. "I never cared much for prunes after that," he quipped later.

To amuse himself when he wasn't watching for fires, Sylvan rigged a long pole with a string noose on the end and snared lizards that sunned themselves on rocks in front of his cabin. He boxed up 20 of the reptiles to ship to Moline, hoping that the specimens would help him to get a good grade from Dr. Joseph E. Guthrie, his wildlife professor at Iowa State. The lizards endured the packhorse trip down the mountain and the train ride to Illinois with no problem. But when the mysterious package was delivered to Sylvan's home in Moline and his mother innocently opened the box, the lizards erupted from the container. Myrtle screamed for the mailman, who helped her to kill "every danged one of them," Sylvan lamented.

When he wasn't lassoing lizards, Sylvan sometimes serenaded the forest wildlife with the accordion his father had shipped to him. The critters probably didn't notice the instrument's missing notes, which were casualties of its trip up the mountain by horseback. Sylvan also plucked out songs on the mandolin that his father had used when courting his mother in southern Illinois. The old mandolin survived the Windy Camp trip and still is a family heirloom.

Sylvan's colleagues on other lookout towers, which were scattered throughout the forest, often competed to be the first to detect the smoke of a fire. Sylvan tallied 44 "smokes" that summer. On slow days the lookouts sometimes talked on the field telephones, catching up on news of the outside world. Sylvan especially remembered a chat with fellow lookout Jim Thorpe, the former Olympic athlete.

Mostly, Sylvan was alone on the mountain. "I kind of enjoyed it," he reflected later. "One thing I would recommend to anybody, if they want to get acquainted with themselves, is to go up there… go out someplace like that and be alone for three months, like I was."

Sylvan cherished another memory of that summer, too. On the way home, while he was hitching a ride in a friend's pickup, the travelers saw an airplane flying through the Columbia River valley. They suddenly realized it was *The Spirit of St. Louis*, piloted by Charles Lindbergh. "Lucky Lindy," who was on a barnstorming tour of the country after his historic transatlantic flight, dipped his wings, waving back at the excited onlookers.

Back in Ames, life at Iowa State apparently seemed too civilized for Sylvan. He and a friend left the fraternity house and lived in a tent near the campus for the spring quarter of 1928. The students occasionally showered in the school gym. Sylvan's son Tom later chuckled about his "cheapskate" father's scheme to save money on housing costs.

Sylvan as a student at Iowa State College in the late 1920s.

The need for money, plus his mother's pleas to have him stay near their home in Moline, persuaded Sylvan to forgo an outdoor experience in the summer of 1928. His father, who worked at the Yellow Sleeve Valve Engine Works, got his son a well-paying job on the assembly line building engines.

He worked long hours — 6 a.m. to 6 p.m. six days a week — but wages were good enough to help Sylvan buy his first car, a 1924 Model T touring car. He paid $65 cash for the beat-up Ford, got a brief driving lesson from the dealer, then drove the jalopy home.

But no college student wants to drive an ordinary car. Sylvan spruced up his vehicle with a paint job, starting with red wheels. He daubed dark green spots on the light green body. "Kind of like a spotted hyena," he mused. Some people thought the vehicle looked more like a frog. It became known thereafter as "the Frog Car."

Sylvan had to hand-crank the engine because the car had no battery or starter. At first, the Model T had a top, which Sylvan later discarded. No one could remember what became of the hood. The back seat also disappeared, but Sylvan improvised by substituting a log. He lost count of the number of cracked radiators he replaced after forgetting to drain the water on cold nights. When the brakes gave out, Sylvan sometimes stopped by steering the front wheels against a curb.

Geneva, Dorothy, and Myrtle once borrowed the car for the 270-mile trip from Moline to Mount Vernon, Illinois, to see relatives. During a storm Geneva stood on the running board holding an umbrella to keep the rain from drowning the engine. They periodically stopped to haul water from creeks to fill the holey radiator. They used 12 quarts of oil. At nearly every service station they bought more oil to add to the leaking crankcase, which they'd patched with chewing gum. Because the car had no horn, Geneva brought along a Ludwig Song Whistle, which had a piercing sound that sometimes startled other drivers or pedestrians.

During the 1928 summer at Yellow Sleeve, Sylvan somehow found the time and money to take flying lessons. That decision would profoundly shape the rest of his life. He soloed at the Moline airport in a Lincoln Standard biplane, although it was more than a decade before he earned his pilot's license.

The following summer, 1929, Sylvan wandered once more. He joined a forestry crew near Cleveland, Ohio, fighting an invasion of Japanese beetles. The job hardly qualified as an "adventure," but at least Sylvan had the satisfaction of working in the woods.

Back at Iowa State for his senior year, Sylvan was elected president of the college's Forestry Club. That display of respect and admiration from his peers would continue with similar honors throughout his life.

But Sylvan's popularity didn't necessarily help him with his studies. He struggled with math and chemistry and had to repeat classes in both subjects. He finally persuaded his advisors to let him substitute a psychology course and an extemporaneous speaking class for two other chemistry requirements.

Sylvan did better with plant taxonomy, botany, principles of general ecology, and lumbering, among other studies expected of forestry majors. With the credits he had earned for forestry summer camp during his freshman year, Sylvan managed to graduate in only four-and-one-half years. Some "professional students" in recent years would have been envious.

Sylvan's college career included a stint in the Reserve Officer Training Corps (ROTC), which at that time was a requirement for every male student. The cadets participated in field artillery drills and basic cavalry instruction. Like most college students, Sylvan probably never dreamed he would have to use that military training.

Romance also blossomed on the Ames campus. A dark-haired home economics major named Beulah Skeie caught Sylvan's eye by checking out dozens of books from the college library, where he worked. A Story County farm girl, Beulah was five years younger than Sylvan and had been a star basketball player at Randall High School.

On their first date — the annual forestry student "hoedown" — Sylvan tried to impress Beulah by firing his pistol into the air. Many of the students brought pistols or shotguns loaded with blanks, and they amused themselves by shooting to scare people. "It was a pretty rough deal," he admitted sheepishly. The event became known informally as "the Brawl," much to the displeasure of college officials. "There may have been parties at which somebody had more fun with fewer people killed, but not right here in Ames," said an irreverent note in *The Ames Forester*, the forestry department's student publication.

But Beulah wasn't scared; she was charmed. "Can he dance?" she wrote in a letter to a friend. "He can dance!" The couple continued to date, then eloped and married in Boone on March 1, 1930. His forestry friends joked that Sylvan had been afflicted with *"Pernicious cupiditis."* A commentary in *The Ames Forester* acknowledged: "He had been showing a weakness for the disease for some time."

In that era, Iowa State students were forbidden to marry, so Beulah

In 1928 Sylvan paid $65 for a 1924 Ford Model T touring car. After he painted it light green with dark green spots, it became "the Frog Car."

had to leave school. Sylvan was allowed to complete his senior year. The newlyweds lived with Beulah's parents on the family farm, where Sylvan helped with milking and other farm chores before going to classes.

Sylvan successfully finished his studies and received a Bachelor of Science degree in forestry in June 1930. Like most of the 16 other forestry graduates, he left college dreaming of a career as a forest ranger.

The annual forestry student "hoedown" at Iowa State College — Sylvan and Beulah in the center.

CHAPTER 5

1930s STRUGGLES

"ANOTHER DAY OLDER AND DEEPER IN DEBT . . ."

No job. No money. Drought. Depression. The hardships of the early 1930s plagued the American people, and Sylvan did not escape. Even so, he started the decade on a happy note, with his Iowa State College forestry degree in hand and his bride at his side.

The reality of hard times quickly set in, however. Despite his college education, Sylvan couldn't find a permanent job. He had to settle for a $100 per month summer surveying job with the Land Economic Survey in northern Wisconsin. Sylvan and his coworkers struggled through tangles of downed trees, trying to locate boundaries of cut-over tracts of timber and to identify remaining tree species.

The lands had reverted to local governments after timber companies had cut most of the big, valuable pines in the mid to late 1800s. Many of those old-growth trees had been floated down the Mississippi River to Iowa and Illinois, where they helped to build barns and farmhouses.

Sylvan relished working in the woods — even if much of the forest had been ravaged by the cut-and-run loggers. "There was still beautiful country, even though it had been completely cut over," Sylvan recalled years later. Although he often had to bushwhack through white cedar swamps or scrubby stands of jack pine or brush left after clear cuts, Sylvan nevertheless was in awe of his surroundings. He studied pileated woodpeckers that hammered on dead pines, admired the occasional patch of big trees that loggers had missed, and puzzled at magnetic rock formations that sometimes spun his compass needle.

The abundance of porcupines fascinated him. When Beulah's family came for a visit, Sylvan used his suspenders to lasso a young porky for the Skeies to take home to show their Iowa friends. (He later regretted having displaced the animal from its North Woods home — and the fact that it quilled the family's unsuspecting farm dog.)

Sylvan found excitement in exploring the wild land, even though it meant days of separation from Beulah, who was pregnant with their first child. Although Beulah at first stayed with Sylvan in Loretta, Wisconsin, and several nearby towns, she moved to a small apartment in Duluth when Sylvan's crew began living in a tent camp. On weekends Sylvan would drive the old Model T Frog Car about 60 miles over forest trails and primitive roads into Duluth for a short stay.

Once, heading back to camp late at night, he nursed the car down a winding forest road in a fierce thunderstorm. Lightning provided more illumination than the Model T's feeble lights, which dimmed as the car slowed and brightened only when he raced the engine. Unfortunately, the aging car had no top, so he was at the mercy of the downpour. "It was another impossible situation," he recalled wryly. "That was a night I'll never forget, because it was one I don't ever expect to go through again!"

Sylvan had another close call that summer, when he was poked in the eye by a broken branch. "I thought I was blind," he said. In pain and barely able to see, he walked five miles through the woods to his camp for help. "I had a heck of a time getting out," he recalled. The injury healed without major damage, but for the rest of his life he occasionally was bothered by scar tissue on his eye.

By November snow flurries began falling on the surveyors. Darkness came early. Sylvan and his companions spent the cold, gray evenings in their cramped tents, playing poker around a woodstove. Yet, Sylvan lamented the end of the work season, despite its long hours and primitive conditions. He'd been at home in the North Woods.

"That was a great summer," he said later. "We all felt kind of a little sad that we were leaving, because we'd worked all six months with those particular guys, and we'd all been up in the woods together," he said.

Worse yet, Sylvan again was without a job to support himself, Beulah, and their soon-to-be-born baby. Struggling to make a living for his family, Sylvan looked for work in Duluth — but the search was in vain. He finally accepted a friend's offer to buy the old Frog Car for $10. Even in the Depression, $10 wouldn't last long. With winter upon them, Sylvan and Beulah boarded a bus and headed toward Iowa.

In the Twin Cities, Sylvan again inquired about jobs — with no luck. But the couple did find reason to celebrate. Their son, Ramon, was born in

Saint Paul on November 24, 1930. The relatives back in Iowa learned of the baby's birth when Beulah's sister Olive read a letter from Beulah at the Skeie Thanksgiving dinner a few days later.

With no means of support for his wife and infant son, Sylvan agreed that his family should move in with Beulah's parents on the farm at Story City. He helped to milk cows, pick corn, and do other farm work. In retrospect, Sylvan said, the experience helped him to relate to the farmers he eventually worked with in his Soil Conservation Service job. "I am an Iowa farmer," he declared!

Sylan as a young father with son Ramon, 1931.

Then he heard of a job as a milk delivery truck driver in his hometown of Moline. Sylvan, Beulah, and baby Ramon moved in with his mother, but the job turned out to be a nightmare. It took Sylvan only a couple of days to tire of getting up at 1 a.m. to go to work. "That got awful old real quick," he joked later.

Beulah shared the frustration. Eager to help her family, she enrolled in nursing school at East Moline State Hospital. Myrtle agreed to baby-sit Ramon while Beulah was in class. But the young mother soon found that the rigors of nurse's training and the demands of caring for and nursing an infant were more than she'd bargained for. She left school so she could focus on raising the baby.

Discouraged by the setbacks, Sylvan turned to Prof Mac, who did his best to buoy the spirits of his former student. The head of the Iowa State College forestry department suggested that his youthful friend grow a mustache to help him look older. And he urged Sylvan to look for work related to forestry, to bolster his experience. The other jobs held no future, Prof Mac told Sylvan. "You're trained to be a forester."

That said, the professor helped to open the door on what turned out to be a lifelong conservation career for Sylvan. MacDonald found Sylvan a part-time job assisting Iowa State College's extension forester, I. T. Bodie. For several months Sylvan traveled the state, laying out windbreaks and helping farmers to plant the trees.

When spring tree-planting season ended, Sylvan again was unemployed. For a time he cultivated corn on his in-laws' farm — but Sylvan still longed for the West and the mountains. Leaving Beulah and Ramon at the farm, he hopped freight trains and hitchhiked his way to the U. S. Forest Service regional headquarters in Missoula, Montana. Summer's heat and lightning had brought on the fire season; he knew he could find work as a firefighter.

When Forest Service officials learned of Sylvan's college training, they said he deserved better than to become a smoke eater. Instead, they offered him a position as a timekeeper, logging the hours of the other firefighters. He spent the rest of the summer on three fires in the rugged mountains of the Beaverhead, Salmon, Deer Lodge, and St. Joe National Forests in northern Idaho and Montana.

On the St. Joe fire, Sylvan was assigned to a crew of about 50 men — some of whom had been forced into service by law officers. Trucks hauling the unenthusiastic fire crew left Missoula at about midnight, then dropped the men at a trailhead well before daylight. "It was black," Sylvan said. "We couldn't see anything."

Sylvan spent the rest of that night and until 9 p.m. the next day hiking 40 miles to the fire site, outdistancing most of his ragtag companions. The trail ended on the banks of the St. Joe River, where Sylvan could see the main firefighter camp on the other side. He shouted to the people in the camp, who urged him to come across. Warily, he waded the cold, swift water in the darkness, then slumped down beside the campfire to dry out.

"Well, you must be hungry," the ranger declared, as he cooked a batch of pancakes over the coals. Tired and wet, Sylvan devoured the pancakes — then promptly fell asleep on the rocks beside the mountain stream.

For the next few weeks Sylvan tallied the workers' hours and tended a small store where the men could get tobacco, socks, gloves, and other goods. He also witnessed some of the earliest attempts to use airplanes to aid in fighting forest fires. Forest Service officials attempted to transport axes, saws, and other firefighting tools to remote sites by dropping bundles of equipment from low-flying planes. But the fall broke the handles of all of the axes and shovels and kinked the saws, so the crews realized they needed to devise a way to use parachutes. Meanwhile, they went back to deliveries by packhorses or mules.

In his free time Sylvan practiced throwing a double-bitted ax at a dead tree.

In 1932, Sylvan (left) worked with U. S. Forest Service crews in the mountains of northern Idaho.

"After a while I got so I could stick it every time," he boasted. He felt so confident that he almost tried to kill a black bear that frequented the camp's garbage dump. "I'm close enough I can swing back and split his skull open," Sylvan figured, as he watched the bear feasting on leftovers from the camp kitchen. "I thought I could do it, and I toyed with that idea for a while, but I finally dismissed it," he reflected. "So I made another decision there that was a survival decision."

A colleague found out about bears the hard way, when he tried to pick up a cub that was walking gingerly through hot ashes near the fire line. "The cub bear just stood up on its hind legs and swatted him and knocked him down," Sylvan laughed. "He learned that you don't mess around with even little cub bears!"

Fall rains ended the fire season, putting Sylvan and his crew out of work. They walked out of the mountains, following the river downstream to St. Mary's, Idaho. Sylvan caught a freight train to Iowa for a reunion with Beulah and Ramon on the Skeie farm.

Jobless once again, Sylvan vowed to find a way to provide for his family. Hitchhiking and carrying his sleeping bag, he headed for Arkansas, following rumors of forestry jobs. After an encounter with a hungry "crowd" of bedbugs in a shabby rooming house along the way, Sylvan slept outdoors on the ground for the rest of the trip.

At last, near Texarkana, in the far southwestern corner of Arkansas, he got a job marking timber at about $2 per day. The company even arranged for room and board for $1.50 per day at a little hotel in a nearby town. But after a couple of weeks, with several days off because of the rain, Sylvan learned that he was 50 cents in the hole. He owed more than he'd earned.

"Another day older and deeper in debt," he said, recalling the words of a popular song. "Well, I found out firsthand how that works," he said, "how the poor people can never get anywhere. They never get a chance." Sylvan left his backpack for collateral, hitchhiked home, then sent back the money he owed to the "company store."

Back in Iowa, Sylvan kept searching for work. The owner of the Grand Market grocery in Davenport promised steady work at $15 per week. Sylvan accepted, hoping for some financial stability. But the fickle grocer laid off his young helper when business slowed after Christmas. Beulah found part-time work as an elevator operator to help pay the bills.

Luckily, his windbreak-planting experience the year before had opened the door for Sylvan to move into another temporary job as an extension forester. He spent part of the winter and early spring drawing plans for more windbreaks and helping farmers to manage woodlots and plant trees for erosion control.

When that job ended in June, Sylvan decided once again to head west, where he could work on a "blister rust" crew fighting a destructive disease that was killing white pine trees in northern Idaho. He hopped a freight bound for the mountains. In western Montana Sylvan jumped off when the train slowed on a sharp curve, then he hiked a narrow trail up a steep valley to the camp where he was to work. The wearisome job consisted of finding and grubbing out gooseberry or currant bushes that played host to the white pine blister rust fungus.

That work lasted into the fall, when Sylvan got a telegram announcing that Beulah had given birth to Marilyn on September 23, 1932, at the farm in Iowa. Sylvan celebrated briefly with some bootleg wine a coworker had made from peach preserves. Then he caught freight trains east for a reunion with his wife, son, and new daughter at the Skeie farm.

Once more he helped with fall corn-picking, then returned to the temporary winter job as an extension forester planning windbreaks. At least he was working, so he was better off than millions of other Americans who remained jobless during the depths of the Great Depression.

CHAPTER 6

CCC

"THAT WAS THE BEGINNING OF A TERRIFIC CONSERVATION IDEA..."

By November 1932 the winds of change were blowing across the country, and Sylvan's luck would change with them. With the election of Franklin D. Roosevelt, and a series of "New Deal" programs, people grew more optimistic.

One of Roosevelt's first acts was to establish the Civilian Conservation Corps (CCC), a program known mostly for putting people to work to improve parks and public lands. But Sylvan's Iowa State College forestry professor thought the conservation principles should apply to farmland, as well. Why not plant trees on private lands for windbreaks or to slow the

"There were gullies everyplace," Sylvan recalled, describing the situation facing Civilian Conservation Corps (CCC) workers in southern Iowa.

Camp Superintendent Sylvan T. Runkel (right center, second row) is surrounded by most of th

disastrous rate of erosion? Prof Mac had promoted this approach for years, sometimes taking students to southern Iowa to help plant trees on rolling fields. In 1929 Sylvan and his classmates had worked with MacDonald on several such conservation projects near Chariton and Albia.

MacDonald drew up a proposal for 30-plus CCC camps to work on private land conservation in Iowa. He outlined the value of conservation and a conservation ethic not only to the individual landowner and the resources, but also to society as a whole. Then MacDonald and Iowa Lieutenant Governor Nels Kraschel rode a train to Washington, D. C., confident they could sell the idea to Roosevelt.

"It wasn't just a benefit to the farmer, it was to the benefit of the whole country if you stopped erosion on the land," said Sylvan, repeating the lessons he'd learned from Prof Mac. "Like Patrick Henry said, 'He is the

...ther "boys" he supervised in Iowa's first CCC camp at Albia in 1933.

greatest patriot who saves the most gullies,'" Sylvan declared.

The Iowans didn't get to see FDR, but they did get an appointment with Robert Fechner, director of the newly created Emergency Conservation Work (ECW) program. As Sylvan retold the story years later, MacDonald made his pitch, then waited only a few minutes before Fechner brought the news from a conference with Roosevelt. "That's just what the president has been looking for — to work these people on private land on conservation work that they need to do," said Sylvan, quoting Fechner's enthusiastic response.

The Dust Bowl of the Southwest and Great Plains clearly had the bureaucrats worried, Sylvan said. When topsoil blown from Texas and Oklahoma fell as red rain on Washington, D. C., "I think that kind of jarred 'em into really getting these programs going," he said.

Iowa became the first state to use CCC crews on private land. MacDonald was appointed state director of the Emergency Conservation Work program, which was charged with setting up the project. There would be CCC camps across the state, administered by the U. S. Army, but with work directed by civilians. And what better choice for the first camp superintendent than Sylvan T. Runkel, one of MacDonald's favorite former students?

The job got Sylvan a big pay raise — all the way up to $170 a month, compared with the $120 monthly salary as an extension forester. Significantly, Camp Superintendent Runkel spent part of his hard-earned pay on a new uniform. He especially prized the broad-brimmed Stetson ranger hat, which later became Sylvan's "old naturalist" trademark.

In May 1933 MacDonald dispatched Sylvan to the town of Albia and Monroe County, in the same area where the young forester had helped to plant trees as an Iowa State College class project a few years before. Sylvan quickly lined up two dozen farmers who agreed to have the government do free conservation work on their land.

"There was an awfully lot of erosion," Sylvan recalled. "Boy, that used to be terrible-looking down there to drive through the country. There were gullies everyplace."

Sylvan was eager to begin what would be a lifelong fight to save the soil, but he needed more than just a good idea. He had to start by buying some basic tools. At Harper-McIntire, a wholesale hardware store in Ottumwa, the astounded owners gladly filled Sylvan's CCC order for several hundred axes, shovels, pickaxes, saws, hammers, and other gear. With almost no sales during the bleak Depression years, the proprietors even agreed to charge the $600 purchase to Uncle Sam.

When the 200 CCC "boys" arrived at Albia, they camped in the city park. Eight or 10 men would crowd into a pyramid tent pitched on a wooden platform. They slept on cots and got heat from a sheet iron stove that burned wood or coal. A wood-fired boiler provided a little hot water — first come, first served — for a shower house. Luckily, the crews started work in May, with the coolest weather behind them. Army officers supervised the camps, seeing that the boys got food, housing, clothing, medical care, and discipline. Sylvan and his assistant leaders directed the crews during the workday.

Not only did Sylvan have to make all the arrangements for the erosion control projects, but often he and his assistants — "local experience men," or LEMs — had to teach the CCC crews how to perform simple tasks such as building fence or using an ax or saw or posthole digger. Many of the disadvantaged youths had never held a job; they had no idea how to use simple hand tools. "Some of them weren't very far up on the educational ladder," Sylvan observed.

It was a learning experience for Sylvan, too. Although he'd never actually built a "check dam" before, he took his foremen into the field and showed them how to use the structures to restore eroding gullies. Working in groups of about 40 boys each, the CCC crews hauled rock or brush to fill woven wire cages in the ditches. They also cut trees, which they used to make fence posts or to build log dams. Then they planted trees to hold the bare soil and built fences to protect the trees and to keep livestock from trampling the gully banks.

The crews discovered that they also must attack the source of the erosion. "Any big program when you start out like that you've got to learn," Sylvan acknowledged. "What they needed to do was farm the field in such a way that the water didn't cause a gully," he said. "If you get something that holds the water up there, you don't need to worry about the gully. It'll soak the water in up where it falls.

"So that's when they started doing more of the terracing and contouring and strip-cropping," Sylvan said, "and that got the people aware of it and they could see what you did to control erosion. We got

CCC workers in the 1930s used rocks, logs, wire, and shovels to build erosion-control barriers. (Photo courtesy Iowa Department of Natural Resources, CCC Museum)

CIVILIAN CONSERVATION CORPS
1933   1942
CCC
U S
1933 · 60TH ANNIVERSARY · 1993

people interested; that was the important thing," he said. "People started thinking about erosion on the fields" — and the CCC began to attack the problem. "The CCC camps were really the big push that got all of this sort of thing going," he said. "That was the beginning of a terrific conservation idea that the whole country is aware of now." Other CCC crews spread lime on farm fields, loading and unloading horse-drawn wagons with shovels. Men from several camps worked in state parks, constructing lakes and buildings that still distinguish Iowa's park system.

Some crews also were assigned to grub out and destroy gooseberry bushes, which are host plants for white pine blister rust. Foresters feared the fungal disease would kill white pine trees that the CCC boys were planting. The CCC crews and other workers spent countless hours unsuccessfully trying to eradicate gooseberries, only to learn later that the rust did not survive the warm climate of southern Iowa.

Sylvan directed the Albia CCC camp for six months. When the crew was transferred to Council Bluffs, Prof Mac tapped Sylvan to become a forestry supervisor for about 30 camps in Iowa and Missouri. Sylvan traveled most of northeastern and southern Iowa and northern Missouri, giving tree-planting demonstrations to CCC crews and to farmers. He also helped to choose sites for additional camps, including those at Sigourney, Iowa, and Leon, Iowa.

His demanding assignment meant that Sylvan sometimes would leave Ames before 6 a.m. to drive to Shenandoah, Waukon, or other corners of the state. He then might conduct field demonstrations or inspections for several days. He stayed overnight at CCC camps or at hotels. In Dubuque, Iowa, the Hotel Canfield charged $1.25 per night. When he traveled to Bethany, Missouri, he could get a room at a tourist camp for $1.

Sylvan seldom let adverse weather or poor roads affect his travel schedule. After a severe ice storm in the winter of 1933 to 1934, he

SYLVAN T. RUNKEL

strapped on ice skates to reach the CCC crews working in the woods near Cresco, Iowa.

Summer weather wasn't much better. "Those were bad years to get anything growing," Sylvan said. "Nineteen-thirty-three and 1934 were just awful, and 1936 wasn't much better. It was terribly dry and terribly hot. That was the time of chinch bugs, and they had grasshoppers, too."

For a year and a half Sylvan supervised CCC forestry operations, traveling throughout the state to teach tree-planting and forest-management skills to supervisors and workers in other camps. He also taught fire-fighting techniques, drawing on his experience from the western states. He continued the contacts with CCC camps even after his job was switched to the Soil Conservation Service (SCS) in 1935.

Despite their far-flung and sometimes isolated locations around the state, the CCC crews developed a lasting camaraderie. As tokens of friendship, Sylvan joked, they'd sometimes mail each other packages of horse manure — C.O.D.

At its peak in 1935 the CCC operated 46 camps in Iowa. During the 10 years of the program, from 1933 through 1942, more than 46,000 unemployed or disadvantaged young men worked on CCC projects in the state. The camps aided the conservation effort, helped workers to get through tough times, and boosted local economies with federal dollars. Sylvan believed that workers at the camps who later served in World War II also made better soldiers, because they'd had a taste of military regimentation.

From his first days with the CCC, Sylvan felt a real satisfaction in doing work that could have an impact on the land. In later years he delighted in showing people the wildlife plantings, erosion control dams, or contour strips that he had helped farmers to install. He lamented changes in farming practices that sometimes destroyed his work, leaving the soil vulnerable to erosion. He also recognized the growing awareness of the importance of soil conservation.

"After they worked so long and got people acquainted with conservation and what they ought to do on conserving their farms, they got it spread around," he said. Neighbors learned from neighbors.

"We started out as 'gully pluggers,'" Sylvan later wrote of his CCC experiences. "We have progressed to where we are concerned with the health of the complete environment! At the center of a livable environment is the soil! Soil — placenta of life that both nourishes and absorbs life. When we're working with the soil, we're working with Life itself!"

The CCC marked a giant step forward for conservation in general, and the beginning of his own career devoted to protecting our natural resources, Sylvan reflected. "From then on, my life has been founded on conservation," he said. "Everybody when they first got the job they thought, well, this is a six-months job — and it ended up being a lifetime job for a lot of people, like me."

CHAPTER 7

EARLY DAYS AT SCS

"HE . . . CERTAINLY PUSHED THE ENVELOPE OF LIFE . . ."

When his job was transferred to the newly formed U. S. Soil Conservation Service (SCS) in 1935, Sylvan's duties at first mirrored his role with the CCC camps: supervising forestry work to aid in soil conservation. Before long, his mission broadened to reflect the philosophy of Hugh Hammond Bennett, the first director of the SCS. Bennett, who had persuaded Congress to rename the Soil Erosion Service and move it from the Department of the Interior to the Department of Agriculture, was known as a relentless crusader for conservation.

Sylvan admired Bennett — a burly and compassionate man who loved to meet farmers, swap stories, and get a feel for their land. Bennett preached the value of a "whole farm conservation plan" that considered the best use for every acre — crop field, woodlot, or wildlife habitat. And

Contour plowing was a relatively new idea when Sylvan began teaching it as a U. S. Soil Conservation Service employee in the 1930s.

Sylvan and Beulah with Ramon and Marilyn in the mid-1930s.

people were a major part of the picture. "When you're taking care of the land, you're taking care of the landowner," Bennett believed.

A 1936 book, *Rich Land, Poor Land*, by Stuart Chase, also reinforced Sylvan's zeal for protecting the land. Sylvan took to heart Chase's premise that the quality of a civilization depended on stewardship of natural resources.

Energized by those conservation messages, Sylvan helped farmers to learn to plant on the contour, seed erodible fields, plant trees, and fence woodlands to protect them from livestock. As heavy equipment became more available, he advocated the construction and management of farm ponds, as well. Often, education was the biggest part of the job. Some landowners at first scoffed at the idea of contours or terracing, which they called "snake farming."

Sylvan took dozens of photos, then put together slide programs to show to farmers. His son Ramon remembers the whole family serving as a test audience when Sylvan practiced his slide shows. Sylvan also gave frequent radio interviews to plant the idea of conservation in his listeners' minds. He wrote regular newspaper columns on topics ranging from meadowlarks to tree planting to contour farming.

In addition to the challenge of the workload, Sylvan had to adjust to a succession of new assignments. For several months he commuted to the Bethany, Missouri, SCS office, while his family still lived in Ames. He also spent almost a year working out of the Knoxville, Iowa, office.

A two-week period in May 1935 illustrates his hectic pace and Sylvan's commitment to his job. According to his journal, Sylvan left Ames on Monday, then made field inspections near the Iowa cities of Waterloo, Cresco, McGregor, Cedar Rapids, Solon, and Sigourney before returning to Ames. Late Thursday night, he drove to Sioux City for two days at a wildlife conference. He got home to Ames at 11 p.m. Saturday, had a brief rest Sunday, then left again at 5 a.m. Monday to drive to Bethany, Missouri, for the week. He returned home the following Saturday afternoon.

We may not want to imagine what the driving was like on Sylvan's many trips. Iowa's network of paved roads was expanding, but many of the routes were narrow and curbed. Even the best highways passed through many small towns and sometimes wound through the hills. The state had not yet imposed a speed limit, so "wide open" became the standard for some drivers. Sylvan was no exception. He liked to drive fast in his 1933 Ford V-8, which he'd bought with paychecks from his CCC job. He test-drove the car near Albia and was so impressed with the power going up the southern Iowa hills that he immediately went back to the dealer and traded in the old Model A he'd been driving.

While Sylvan was on the road, the government paid him $3.60 per day expenses and 5 cents per mile if he drove his own car. At least that was the rate in early 1935. By the end of that year, with the Depression still pinching the American economy, the rates were lowered to $3 per day and 4 cents per mile.

With all his travels to give programs and demonstrations at CCC camps, Sylvan often had to work Saturdays or evenings to keep up with office chores. And with the country still trying to rebound from the decade's economic woes, he had to take an 18 percent pay cut — from $3,200 per year down to $2,600 per year — between 1937 and 1940. Like most Americans of the era, he accepted the long hours, frequent transfers, and modest salary as small prices to pay for a secure position.

Despite the hard times, Sylvan's journal often mentioned cheerful diversions such as music. The whole family sometimes broke into song, whether riding in the car or gathered in the living room while Sylvan played the piano and composed humorous lyrics. "We had fun with music," said Ramon.

Sylvan and Beulah frequently attended movies to see such rising stars as Clark Gable and Mae West. Sometimes they drove from Ames to Des Moines to see auto shows or musicals. After church on Sundays

Sylvan took his family picnicking, ice-skating, roller-skating, or sledding. In 1934 Sylvan and Beulah took Sylvan's sisters and his mother to the World's Fair in Chicago.

In 1935 Sylvan and Beulah drove to Callander, Ontario, to see the famous Dionne quintuplets, who had been born the year before. They first stopped in Moline, where Sylvan's sister Dorothy impulsively decided to go along. When they returned, Sylvan persuaded Dorothy to stay with his family in Ames to attend Iowa State.

Sylvan also squeezed in time to hunt and fish, savoring the Iowa outdoors. He spent some summer nights catfishing on the Raccoon River, and looked forward to Armistice Day pheasant and duck hunts "up north" at a friend's farm near Emmetsburg. He considered hunting another way to connect to the land.

After a visit to a CCC camp at Sigourney, Sylvan and some of the other employees decided to go 'coon hunting. When they shot a raccoon, Sylvan kept the pelt to make a coonskin cap. "You looked real good wearing it," his fellow hunter insisted. (The family still has the cap.)

Sylvan seldom missed an Iowa State home football game. He began taking Ramon to the games when his son was only 5 or 6 years old. Although football was his favorite spectator sport, Sylvan occasionally listened to World Series baseball games on his car radio — and lamented yet another victory by the New York Yankees.

Sylvan's thirst for adventure had not waned. In 1936 he and a friend attempted to scale the Grand Teton. Their first effort failed, but Sylvan was hooked on mountain climbing. He reached the peak the following year with Floyd Harrison, an SCS colleague.

In 1937 when the SCS assigned him to work in Greenfield, Iowa, the family moved from Ames. At their new home, Sylvan occasionally played a round of golf, went bowling, played tennis, or helped a friend work on his Harley Davidson motorcycle. He also joined the Masonic Lodge, sang in the church choir, and delighted in being a dad to Ramon and Marilyn. He would read wildlife books, such as Ernest Thompson Seton's classic series on the lives of game animals, then re-tell animal stories to the youngsters. Beulah sometimes invited the children's schoolteachers to the Runkel home for dinner.

In February 1938 Sylvan persuaded his bosses that he should attend the North American Wildlife Conference in Baltimore. At the meeting he met a fellow forester named Aldo Leopold more than a decade before

A 1930s photo of Sylvan on a Loess Hills overlook (probably at Waubonsie State Park, near Hamburg, Iowa) illustrates his long-standing love of the hills.

Leopold's classic book, *A Sand County Almanac*, was published. He talked with conservationist J. N. "Ding" Darling, *The Des Moines Register's* Pulitzer Prize-winning cartoonist, creator of the first federal duck stamp, and former director of the U. S. Biological Survey. The conference also included a lively discussion on the federal Pittman-Robertson wildlife restoration bill, which passed in 1937 and went into effect in 1938. The landmark legislation, which still is in place today, provided money for wildlife management by taxing guns and ammunition.

But Sylvan was not content merely to go to the meeting, rub elbows with important people, discuss hot issues, then return home. Instead, he and Beulah and three friends planned an automobile adventure to Niagara Falls, New York City, Washington, D. C., and Baltimore. For a finale, they returned home by way of Miami Beach, the Everglades, Tallahassee, Alabama, Mississippi, and the Mardi Gras in New Orleans.

Headed for home on the last leg of the monthlong working vacation, they stopped in Kansas City to catch a matinee featuring Ginger Rogers and Katharine Hepburn in "Stage Door." They drove back to Greenfield in the dark.

Some of us might need a rest to recover from such a schedule — but not Sylvan. He was ready for more. He busied himself again with a full schedule of talks to high school students, tree-planting demonstrations, and helping farmers to lay out contour strips. In his spare time, Sylvan was planning the next expedition: another mountain-climbing trip to Wyoming.

"He had so much zest for so many aspects of life," said Ramon, recalling his father's example. "He loved to participate and he wanted to learn."

The busy work and family life kept up through transfers to the Marion and Monticello, Iowa, SCS offices in the late '30s and early '40s. Arnie Webster, whose father, Vergil, worked with Sylvan, said his association with the Runkel family shaped his life. The Websters and Runkels frequently picnicked at Thomas Park in Marion, where Sylvan sometimes brought archery equipment and taught the youngsters how to shoot.

"Sylvan was constantly teaching Ramon and Marilyn, including whomever else was present," Webster said. "During hikes he tested us on the types of trees and the multitude of plants we'd see in the woods of Iowa.

"Sylvan was ever the gentle, knowledgeable, easy teacher, whether the subject was nature, demonstrating his Colt Woodsman .22-caliber pistol, and relating his adventures, or looking at the heavens, pointing out stars, and identifying constellations," Webster said. Sylvan also showed the kids how to rig and sail a boat.

"I was ever in awe of the seemingly inexhaustible extent of his daring and expertise," Webster added. "Whatever the subject, he always knew something about it and took time to share." His quiet confidence earned Sylvan the admiration of his many friends, Webster said. "He was very adventurous and obviously a strong leader who certainly pushed the envelope of life."

Sylvan (right) and Floyd Harrison prepare for a Wyoming backpacking trip in the 1930s. (Iowa State University/Special Collections Department)

Indeed, Sylvan enjoyed life — whether he was criss-crossing Iowa to sell farmers on the merits of conservation or teaching his children the joys of nature. The family sometimes camped or hiked at Ledges, Pammel, Backbone, Clear Lake, or other state parks.

When Sylvan found unusual plants or animals — especially snakes — he'd often bring them home to show the children. "Even in kindergarten, Ray and I always were getting to take wonderful examples of nature to school for show and tell," Marilyn said. Once, when Marilyn was sick in bed, Sylvan brought her a large king snake to boost her spirits.

"Snakes were really a big part of my up-bringing," Marilyn recalled. "Sylvan wanted to prove, I think, that girls don't have to scream when they see bugs or see snakes. I can remember being taught how you hold the snake and let it move, and he would have me demonstrate how to let them be your necklace or your belt."

One cool fall day, Sylvan wanted to show off nearly 50 snakes — blue racers, ring-necks, bullsnakes and others — that he'd rescued when their den was destroyed by a limestone quarry. But the lethargic serpents quickly came to life when Sylvan dumped them from a burlap sack in his warm house. "The whole floor was wriggling," laughed Marilyn. Beulah was not so amused. She tried to institute a "no snakes in the house" rule — but it did not last.

Although the decade of the '40s began with this good life and family times, a few clouds already had begun to hang on the horizon. On a hot Saturday evening, August 2, 1941, Sylvan had to face a tragedy that his heroics could not prevent.

While fishing with his boss, Vergil Webster, on the Mississippi River downstream from Lock and Dam 9 north of McGregor, Sylvan heard the frantic screams of several teenagers who were swimming at a beach along the river. A young woman apparently had stepped into a hole and gone under the water, and her companions were trying to save her.

Sylvan, Webster, and a friend managed to pull two boys to safety, and Sylvan yanked off his trousers and dove into the murky river to search for other swimmers. Again and again, Sylvan swam into the depths of treacherous waters. Finally, exhausted from fighting the current, he had to admit defeat. Searchers later found the bodies of the 18-year-old girl and a 15-year-old boy who had drowned trying to save her.

Ramon and Marilyn, who were ages 10 and 8 at the time, never forgot the story of their father's bravery — and his deep, profound sadness at not being able to help the young people who died.

But the drownings paled in comparison with the looming international events that were about to change the entire world even more dramatically than Sylvan could have imagined.

Sylvan (right) and his friend Floyd Harrison on a 1930s canoe trip.

CHAPTER 8

THE WAR

"SYLVAN RUNKEL PAID FOR LIBERTY FOR ALL THE REST OF US WITH EVERY STEP HE TOOK FOR 50 YEARS."

Flight Officer Sylvan T. Runkel U.S. Army Air Corps.

By 1940 Sylvan and his family, like many Americans, had overcome the struggles of the 1930s. Sylvan had a good job with the SCS in the agency's Marion office.

Despite the relatively good life in the United States, political and military unrest had wracked other parts of the world. On September 21, 1938, Sylvan noted the international events in his diary: "Today Czechoslovakia capitulated to Hitler. Shame on you, France and England." He could not understand why world leaders were allowing the German aggression.

A few days later, Sylvan wrote briefly about radio reports of the continuing unrest. "Listen to Hitler orate over the air — wild and excited." The thoughts continued the following day: "Hear [British Prime Minister] Chamberlain's sad speech on war possibilities." Even children could not escape the growing war rhetoric. "Too bad about chocolate-slovakia," said Marilyn, his 6-year-old daughter.

While many Americans wanted to avoid the conflicts, world tensions continued to grow, and politicians debated where it all would lead. The answer came on Sunday, December 7, 1941. While Sylvan was fishing with friends in the Mississippi River at Guttenberg, they heard the news about the Japanese attack on Pearl Harbor. The United States could no longer ignore the turmoil. War had been thrust upon us.

Sylvan's first impulse was to join the battle for freedom, as had his

Sylvan and an Army Air Corps friend.

ancestors in the Revolutionary War, Indian Wars, and the Civil War. His patriotism also had been reinforced by his 1938 visit to Washington, D. C., when he'd seen and heard President Franklin D. Roosevelt give a tribute to Abraham Lincoln at the Lincoln Memorial.

On December 18, 1941, Sylvan went to the Linn County Office of Civilian Defense and volunteered for duty with the Civil Air Patrol. The newly formed agency recruited civilians who might be willing to use private airplanes for military or defense assignments. Sylvan flew a few patrols, but he continued to wrestle with his conscience for several months. Would it be more patriotic to be available as a volunteer pilot and to work with farmers on food production, or to enter the military and join the real fight? In July 1942 the Runkel taste for excitement won out again. Although he was 35 and the father of two children, Sylvan enlisted in the Army Air Corps.

With his college degree he could have received a commission as an officer. But Sylvan would have nothing of that. Since boyhood he had dreamed of being a pilot. He wanted to fly. He'd begun flying lessons in the 1920s, had earned his pilot's license in 1940, and had logged more than 200 hours of flying time.

But the Army wanted young men as airplane pilots — not "old" soldiers like Sylvan. He had to be satisfied with learning to fly a glider. Sylvan became part of what turned out to be an unsuccessful experiment. (After several wartime missions the use of gliders to transport soldiers and materiel was abandoned as impractical.)

Undaunted, Sylvan eagerly accepted the chance to fly — even if it had to be without an engine. He'd been fascinated with gliders for several years after watching flights at Bolling Field on the 1938 trip to Washington, D. C. And he'd read about the aircraft in *Popular Aviation*. Sylvan and the other trainees practiced "dead stick landings" in single engine planes with their engines turned off. The students later flew Piper Cubs, Taylorcrafts, and Aeroncas with their engines removed and a seat added.

Sylvan caught on fast and soon became a glider instructor. He earned the nickname "Pops" from airmen half his age. Lynus Ryan, a fellow pilot who got to know Sylvan because their last names put them side-by-side in roll call, couldn't believe that Sylvan was so much older than his cohorts. "He could have served in a lot of other ways" than volunteering for combat, Ryan said. "He didn't have to do what he did.

"He always was well liked by everybody," Ryan added. "It was just his attitude. He never had a down day, it seemed. He was always cheerful about what was going on, even though some of those experiences — like some of those 20-mile [training] hikes — weren't too pleasant. But he didn't shirk from any of that duty!"

His love of hunting and shooting made Sylvan a crack shot, as well. He qualified as an "expert" with his military .45-caliber pistol and as a "sharpshooter" with the Army's M-1 rifle.

It had to have been an exciting time for Sylvan. He was flying! He criss-crossed the country for two years, serving at bases in Missouri, Ohio, Texas, New Mexico, California, Indiana, Kentucky, North Carolina, and New Jersey. Beulah and the children often stayed with her family on the farm near Story City, but they joined Sylvan when they could. They borrowed a friend's 23-foot house trailer and used Sylvan's 1937 V-8 Ford, nicknamed "The Suzy Q," to pull the tiny mobile home to Fort Sumner, New Mexico, and Victorville, California.

The family tried to take advantage of the travels as a learning experience, with visits to such attractions as Carlsbad Caverns, New Mexico. Ramon and Marilyn especially remember rattlesnake hunts in Texas. Later, when the family was back in Ames, Sylvan sent them a horned toad from New Mexico. "Horny" became the hit of the fourth grade in Marilyn's elementary school.

Young Ramon relished the adventure of seeing the country and associating with soldiers — but Sylvan sternly reminded his son not to glorify war. "An army… has one mission: to kill people," Sylvan told Ramon. "I certainly don't want to kill anybody, but I do think our way of life and the way of life of many people in the world is being threatened. I have to do what I'm doing, but I don't like what I'm doing," Sylvan said. Ramon never forgot that lecture — or his father's "sense of fairness."

Sylvan's military service took on an even more somber mood when the pilots were shipped to Bowman Field, Kentucky, for combat training. The war was intensifying and the Allied invasion to liberate Europe was imminent. Military strategists were studying a plan to use gliders to carry troops behind the lines. And those glider pilots wouldn't have the luxury of staying above the fray. When a glider landed, its crew would have to be ready to fight with grenades, rifles, or bayonets.

At Laurimburg Air Base in Maxton, North Carolina, the pilots practiced eerie night landings guided only by flares. The training was a chilling reminder that their mission was to be deadly serious — and dangerous. Sylvan and his fellow soldiers in the 72nd Squadron of the 434th Troop Carrier Group would carry combat forces into battle.

Yet, the soldiers felt almost privileged as they set out from Camp Kilmer, New Jersey, headed across the Atlantic to Liverpool, England, in May 1944. They sailed on the *Louis Pasteur*, a private French liner that had been pressed into military service. Flight Officer Sylvan T. Runkel and about 300 other glider pilots were assigned to quarters with eight or 10 officers in each room. They ate in the officers' dining room, which featured good food, waiters, and tablecloths. The 6,000 other men on the vessel weren't so lucky. The military was segregated in 1944, and most of the ship's enlisted men were black. They stayed in large rooms with 50 or 60 other soldiers and were allowed on deck only briefly each day.

While in England, Sylvan marveled at the spirit of the British people, who maintained their optimism despite the destruction of their cities by German bombs and the constant threat of more bombing raids. Store windows contained tempting displays of chocolates, although few people could afford to buy candy. Flower vendors received extra gasoline rations because Prime Minister Winston Churchill believed their bouquets might give the British a psychological boost.

At the same time, military officials were preparing for a massive assault that would be unparalleled in terms of the number of people and amount of war machinery involved. One publication described England as "one vast warehouse" of airplanes, tanks, attack vehicles, and

SYLVAN T. RUNKEL

Sylvan photographed a fellow glider pilot on tow during their Army Air Corps training in the early 1940s.

munitions. The soldiers could feel the pressure mounting. Sylvan made several more training flights to get the feel of the British Horsa gliders. Strategists wanted to use the Horsas, which could carry heavier loads, instead of the smaller CG-4 aircraft the American pilots had been flying.

The tensions continued to build. On June 4, 1944, Sylvan and thousands of other servicemen prepared for what was to be one of the biggest and most decisive battles of the war. They waited restlessly while bad weather prolonged the anxiety. Heavy seas and strong winds in the English Channel forced Supreme Allied Commander General Dwight D. Eisenhower to delay the attack.

Finally, late on June 5, word came again: The storm had eased. Forecasters promised a small window of good weather to launch the assault, code-named "Operation Overlord." The time was near. Nobody slept much. Soldiers stocked up on extra ammunition for "Garands," their .30-caliber, eight-shot, M-1 rifles. They stuffed packages of K rations into their knapsacks. Many men strapped combat knives below their knees. Sylvan checked and rechecked his pistol. Smokers and nonsmokers alike took extra cigarettes to use as trading stock with other soldiers or French citizens. They studied their maps one last time, memorizing the sites where they hoped to land. Sylvan's glider sat ready, loaded with communications equipment, a Jeep trailer, two motorcycles, and space for 11 men. For luck, Sylvan had painted the name "Ramon A.," for his son Ramon Allyn, on the nose of the Horsa.

The Allies were counting on surprise. For days they had leaked false messages to confuse the Germans. To add to the deception, they launched balloons and dropped aluminum foil from airplanes far from the intended landing site on the beaches of Normandy. The ruse was so effective that some German commanders did not believe that the invasion had begun, even after the first Allied troops parachuted onto French soil just after midnight on June 6.

The first soldiers met little resistance as they waded ashore at Utah Beach at 6:31 a.m. Several hundred gliders soon followed. Sylvan's squadron was to be the second wave, waiting until just before sundown.

That afternoon dozens of C-47 tow planes and gliders lined up on the runway at Aldermaston, England. Hundreds more prepared to take off from other airfields. Engines were running. Some soldiers were praying. Adrenaline was pumping.

Suddenly a military vehicle raced down the airstrip between the waiting aircraft. "Get out of the gliders!" came the order. There was a hitch in the invasion plan. Allied intelligence had learned that the Germans still held many of the proposed landing fields, which had been booby-trapped to thwart the gliders.

Rather than cancel the attack, officers handed out new orders. The invasion was still on — but the gliders would land at alternate sites.

Sylvan apparently snapped this photo during his glider pilot training at the beginning of World War II.

Because of the change in plans, the pilots realized that they might face crash-landings in small, tree-lined fields, rather than have the luxury of setting down the ponderous Horsa gliders in open farm country.

At about 6:30 p.m. the tow planes roared to life again and accelerated down the runway. Lines of gliders followed obediently, like dogs on leashes. Wave after wave of gliders strung out over southern England as a diversionary tactic before turning east over the channel. Military officials described it as "the most massive towing effort ever conducted." Looking back from his position as the eighth aircraft from the front of the echelon, Sylvan could not see the end of the 50-mile formation of gliders. He shivered at the sight of all that air power — and perhaps at the uncertainty that lay ahead.

The formations of airplanes and gliders headed for France at nearly 150 miles per hour, pushing the safety limits of the gliders, which were designed for slower speeds. As the planes neared the coast, they descended to less than 200 feet to make it harder for German antiaircraft guns to zero in on them.

Sweeping past Utah Beach, then inland just above the treetops, line after line of gliders and tow planes headed over the Normandy mainland. Fighting the natural lift of the wings, Sylvan and pilot Sam Shapiro leaned all their weight on the controls to keep the glider from soaring higher. Sylvan could hear sporadic German small-arms fire and the thunk of bullets piercing the plywood body of the aircraft.

About five miles inland the glider pilots cut loose from the tow planes, after more than two hours aloft. In the early evening light, the men could see lines of trees surrounding their tiny landing fields. With orders to fly straight ahead, lest they crash into other gliders on either side, the men and their now powerless aircraft hurtled toward a hedgerow. Shapiro gave the order to put down the flaps to slow the glider, but it was too late: The Horsa smashed into a stone wall hidden by the trees and brush. "There is no second-guessing on anything like that," Sylvan said later.

Flying at perhaps 80 miles per hour, the glider disintegrated on impact. Shapiro was killed, as were at least two others in the 11-man crew. Sylvan smashed through the front end of the glider, tumbled through the air, and landed more than 50 feet away. Lynus Ryan, who was piloting a glider behind Sylvan's, watched in horror as his friend's aircraft crashed. He radioed for medical help, fearing the worst.

Miraculously, Sylvan survived. The impact knocked him unconscious, smashing the entire left side of his body. His leg was broken in three places, his elbow was fractured, and several teeth were snapped off. With his teeth broken and blood coming from his mouth, Sylvan probably looked like a vampire, he joked later. "It kind of mashed us up a bit," he admitted. "I was in kind of tough shape." But he was alive.

The surviving soldiers tried to tend to their injured buddies and to retrieve the glider's scattered cargo. One motorcycle hung from a tree. Some of the men found the trailer loaded with wire and radio equipment and managed to set up a communications post. The crash scene echoed with the sound of battle as infantrymen from the 101st Airborne and other Allied troops fought the German defenders.

When Sylvan regained consciousness, daylight was fading. "Everything was all confusion," he recalled. "There was lots of shooting going on. You could hear big guns in the distance and explosions and rifle fire here and there and all over — just like a big, heavy Fourth of July celebration going on all through the countryside. That's how it sounded."

Medics found Sylvan and a few other men and moved them into a corner of the field. But a German patrol soon spotted the soldiers and opened fire with automatic pistols. The rapid shots sounded to Sylvan like chattering typewriters. But all he could do was listen helplessly, as the medics shouted in vain, "Medical! Medical!" One of the medics was killed and another was wounded. Although the body of his pilot, Sam Shapiro, partially shielded Sylvan, a German bullet shattered Sylvan's kneecap.

Battered, broken, and bleeding, Sylvan lay semiconscious as the Germans approached. Sylvan fully expected to be shot again, or bayoneted. "I knew I was goin' to get it," he said. But a German soldier — a young man whose face Sylvan never forgot — spared Sylvan. Instead of killing his enemy, the man took Sylvan's watch and left him for dead. Did the soldier see the German name "Runkel" on Sylvan's uniform and feel compassion, or did the trooper simply not want to waste a bullet on someone who seemed doomed to die anyway? Perhaps the German fighter hoped to make more work for the Allies by leaving a wounded man for them to deal with.

Sylvan later voiced sympathy for the German soldiers, who scrambled hysterically around the battlefield. "I doubt if they made it, any of them," he said wistfully. The men who elected not to kill him almost certainly were shot and killed by Allied troops.

Nightfall interrupted the fighting and the battlefield grew quieter. But

Sylvan came home to visit Beulah, Marilyn, and Ramon during his Army Air Corps training from 1942-1944.

then the rain started. Lying on the ground next to his dead flight partner, Sylvan faded in and out of consciousness. Finding a stretcher left by the ill-fated medics, he used his good right arm to pull the canvas over himself to ward off the showers. His body had been shattered — but Sylvan was determined not to die. His mental toughness took over. He also knew his family was praying for him, and for the thousands of other dead and wounded troops who lay bleeding in the dark in the French countryside. "I stayed there all night," Sylvan said whimsically. "Where else would I go?"

When morning broke, Sylvan was amazed to see a young woman walking among the wounded soldiers on the battlefield, giving the men drinks of Calvados, a French apple brandy. The fighting still raged, but the French farm girl had risked her life to help the troops that had come to free her country. As American paratroopers and their Allied friends gained the upper hand later that morning, medical help reached Sylvan. The medics used bunches of hay from the field to devise crude splints for Sylvan's mangled left leg and arm. They put him on a stretcher atop a Jeep and took him to a nearby farmyard that had become a battalion aid station for hundreds of wounded. In a bloody, makeshift operating room in the farmhouse, surgeons were amputating useless limbs. When the doctors

Sylvan and sister Geneva during the war years.

saw the gravity of Sylvan's wounds, however, they transferred him to the nearby beach for evacuation. Luck was with him again. Sylvan believed the farmyard was bombed not long after he left.

Numb from pain and from painkilling drugs, Sylvan nevertheless remained alert enough to observe the chaotic scene on the beach, where he lay with hundreds of other wounded soldiers. In the midst of the confusion, two German fighter planes roared over — only to be met with a fusillade of antiaircraft fire. Helpless to move out of the way, Sylvan feared he might be hit by falling debris from the intense shooting. One plane and its pilot plunged into the ocean. The other German pilot parachuted to earth, where he was captured. The prisoner eventually was shipped to England on the same boat as Sylvan.

Finally, at the end of the second day of the D-Day attack, Sylvan was evacuated from the beach on an amphibious "duck." The craft brought Sylvan and other wounded men out to sea for transfer to an LST (Landing Ship Tank.) A crane lifted his stretcher and swung him over the water between the two boats. He cringed as he thought of the consequences if he fell. What if he had survived the horrific battle, only to be dropped into the sea with his arms and legs strapped at his side? "I was really sweating that one out!" he recalled later.

Safely onboard the LST, Sylvan was placed on a table in the crew's quarters because the ship's deck was filled with wounded. Sailors offered him morphine and words of encouragement. One fellow glider pilot declared that Sylvan was lucky to be wounded and leaving the battle scene. The healthy troops would have to stay to fight again — and perhaps to die. His words were prophetic; the man was killed on a later mission.

The chilling stories of D-Day continue to captivate and horrify the nation more than half a century later. Operation Overlord involved more than 150,000 troops, 10,000 aircraft, and 5,000 ships. About 2,500 Allied soldiers were killed and 9,500 injured. Sylvan remained modest about his role in a battle that was one of the turning points of the war — and perhaps of world history. "I got in on the ground floor," he said matter-of-factly. "It was a great show to watch, but the price of admission was kind of high."

But Sylvan's ordeal continued, even after the "show" was over. All that night and the next day the overloaded ship tossed on the choppy waters of the English Channel. At dusk the craft docked in England, where the wounded soldiers were transferred to the tent shelters of a field hospital. At last doctors could X-ray Sylvan, tend his wounds, set his broken bones, and put casts on his leg and arm. The cast on his left leg reached from his waist to his ankle.

After two or three days at the field hospital, Sylvan went by train to a British hospital, where he stayed for three months. On August 30, 1944 — his 38th birthday — Sylvan was able to share a cake with fellow patients. The dietician just happened to be a family friend from Ames, who arranged for the welcome change from the usual hospital food.

When doctors agreed he was strong enough for more travel, Sylvan was sent to Prestwick, Scotland, to catch a flight back to the States. When the plane stopped in Iceland, the soldiers were offered fresh milk and ice cream — treats that they devoured with gusto. Several of the patients, including Sylvan, paid for their indulgence with digestive upsets that lasted the rest of the trip to Mitchell Field, New Jersey. "It still was worth it," Sylvan laughed later. "We hadn't had any food like that for a long time!"

Sylvan was transferred to Crile Hospital in Cleveland, Ohio. In October 1944, while he lay in his hospital bed, Sylvan first heard the cries of his baby daughter, Karen, over the telephone. Years later Karen (who now uses the name Prasannata) wondered whether there could have been a spiritual connection to her father even before her birth. "Maybe my little soul was over there watching the whole thing," she reflected.

Sylvan's treatment, including about two dozen surgeries on his leg, knee, and mouth, continued for nearly three years. His condition

Daughter Marilyn and Sylvan during his recovery.

gradually improved enough for him to leave the hospital for brief visits to Beulah and the children in Ames, to his mother in Moline, and even to Minnesota. But doctors were not successful in rebuilding his damaged knee. His kneecap had been destroyed and the joint simply could not be restored. When he was transferred to a military hospital in Battle Creek, Michigan, which specialized in amputations, Sylvan feared the worst. Ultimately, doctors saved his leg, but they had to remove a piece of his shinbone and use it to fuse the knee.

To compound his disability, Sylvan suffered recurring bouts with osteomyelitis, a bone infection that apparently was caused by organisms in the straw from which battlefield medics had improvised a splint for his leg. Finally, doctors suppressed the infection by experimenting with massive doses of a new drug whose use was popularized by the war effort. Many wounded soldiers, including Sylvan Runkel, probably owed their lives to the wonders of penicillin.

When he was discharged from the service in August 1947 — more than three years after D-Day — his left leg was slightly shorter than his right and his knee would never flex again. When an SCS coworker once asked him why he limped, Sylvan replied wryly that he was thankful he was limping — it was either be limping or be dead.

"I guess I would be classified as a sidehill gouger," he later joked. "I can walk around a hill one way, but the other way is pretty tough." Sylvan somehow kept his positive outlook, despite his long hospitalization and painful injuries. "What cannot be cured, must be endured," he believed.

Jennie Tweed, an Army nurse who cared for Sylvan at Crile Hospital and became a lifelong friend, described him as "an instant bright light for so many of his fellow comrades." She recalled how "Runk," as his war buddies called him, would lead sing-alongs while playing a piano that had been wheeled in beside his hospital bed. Sometimes he'd use his healthy right arm to reposition the crippled left arm on the keyboard — but the handicap did not detract from the therapeutic music. "Sylvan ignited the joy that was suppressed," Tweed said.

As Sylvan grew stronger, he also played the piano at Crile's Copper Kettle restaurant and bar, nicknamed the "Iron Lung," where the recuperating soldiers gathered for "treatments." Building the morale of others no doubt kept Sylvan's own spirits up as well. And the exercise of playing piano helped to rebuild the strength and agility of his broken left arm. Eventually he regained almost all the function of his arm, although he always carried a bit of French soil imbedded in his knuckle.

Ever looking for the bright side, Sylvan believed his ill-fated crash may have led to improvements in military equipment. U. S. Air Force Colonel Gilmour C. MacDonald, son of Sylvan's Iowa State College forestry professor, cited Sylvan's experience as one of the inspirations behind his invention of a retro-rocket system to slow landing gliders. The thrusters later were adapted to guide intercontinental ballistic missiles.

Sylvan received a Purple Heart and an Air Medal with Bronze Arrowhead for his wartime service. He also may have taken some comfort

Despite his severe injuries on D-Day, Sylvan may have been lucky. Thousands of Allied soldiers are buried in this military cemetery in Normandy.

On a 1979 trip to France, Sylvan visited the grave of Sam Shapiro, the pilot who died in the crash of the men's glider on D-Day, June 6, 1944.

in knowing that other soldiers, and other Americans, recognized and appreciated his sacrifice. "Your World War II heroism made it possible for some of us who came along later in France to land in relative safety," wrote the late Ken Madden, an Iowa Conservation Commission fisheries biologist and ecologist who worked with Sylvan for nearly 30 years.

The late George Knaphus, a close friend and Iowa State University botany professor who fought at the Battle of the Bulge, said his own war experiences paled in comparison to Sylvan's. "I thought I had it tough," Knaphus declared. "But Sylvan Runkel paid for liberty for all the rest of us with every step he took for 50 years."

CHAPTER 9

STARTING ANEW

"HE'D ROLL UP HIS SLEEVES . . ."

After three long years of hospital rooms, pain, and uncertainty, with only a few trips home to see his family, Sylvan at last could come back to Iowa to stay. He received his medical discharge in August 1947, yearning to return to civilian life and to catch up on the adventures and family time he'd missed while in the service and during his recuperation.

Ramon, who was 11 years old when Sylvan enlisted in the Army Air Corps, was now 16 and a gifted athlete on the Ames High School football and track teams. Marilyn, a little girl when her dad went off to war, was now a young woman of 14. And Karen, born just a few months after Sylvan's near-death experience on D-Day, had grown into a lively toddler who needed a father's attention and love.

Sylvan, Beulah, and their children – Ramon, Karen, and Marilyn – posed for this family portrait for their 1948 Christmas card.

Sylvan accepted his war injury and did not expect any sympathy for what he had endured. In fact, he sometimes reflected on how lucky he was to have survived perilous situations in which other people were not so fortunate. He was determined not to let his injury alter his lifestyle. He quickly learned to use his stiff leg to operate the clutch in his cars. He also resumed flying a small plane.

His love of the outdoors and his passion for fishing and hunting remained stronger than ever. In fact, Sylvan's hunting fever almost led to another tragedy before he had recovered from the war. In November 1946, while still wearing a leg brace and on medical leave, he returned to one of his favorite hunting spots, Little Wall Lake near Jewell, Iowa, to hunt waterfowl. He narrowly escaped drowning when strong winds caught his leaky boat as he tried to retrieve a duck.

Sylvan and children Ramon and Karen, 1952.

Nor had Sylvan lost his zeal for exploring wilder places. When some Ames friends invited them to stay at a cabin on Trout Lake, in northern Minnesota, he and Beulah took the children to the scenic, roadless area. Although he still was receiving treatment for his war injuries, Sylvan insisted on rowing a boat six miles to the cabin. He declined the offer of a tow from friends with an outboard motor.

Sylvan thrived on the fresh air and exercise, as he had throughout his life. At Trout Lake Sylvan challenged Ramon to a swimming race to a raft anchored just off shore. Ramon reluctantly agreed, assuming that he could easily outpace a 40-year-old man with a bum leg. But Sylvan won the race to the raft, and his embarrassed son only managed to tie his father on the return swim to shore.

His active lifestyle helped Sylvan to put the war behind him, as did his return to his job with the SCS, where he worked as district conservationist in the Ottumwa office. He could continue to serve his country by spreading the all-important conservation message to farmers.

Although Sylvan could have worked behind a desk, he often avoided his office, preferring one-on-one contact with farmers. He wanted to show them how to get in touch with their land and its variety of "fellow citizens." With Sylvan helping them to prepare conservation plans, farmers learned to look at their farms as living communities, which they wanted to improve and protect.

While Sylvan was headquartered in Ottumwa, his family stayed in Ames so that Ramon could continue to play on the football team. Sylvan left work early every Friday to drive from Ottumwa to Ames to watch his son, an all-conference, 133-pound halfback who often starred in the games.

The busy schedule with family and his SCS job helped Sylvan to grow stronger and readjust to a normal life after his wartime ordeal. At the same time, however, Beulah's health suffered. While Sylvan had been away at war she had contracted undulant fever, apparently from drinking unpasteurized milk from a neighbor's cows. The malady, not uncommon in rural America at the time, periodically left her exhausted and depressed. The usually active, vibrant young mother was frustrated by occasional chills, fever, pains, and weakness that could come and go without warning. Beulah fought the ailment for several years while the disease continued to sap her strength. She died in August 1949.

Once again the Runkel spirit was to be sorely tested. After withstanding the hell of war followed by three years of hospitalization, Sylvan longed to live a happy life with his family. But those dreams were not to be. Now Sylvan had to cope with the anguish of losing his wife — and with the challenges of being a single parent to three growing children who mourned the loss of their mother.

"Dad grieved and really struggled in those years," said Ramon. "I'm sure he went through some emotional ups and downs." To take his mind off his misfortunes, Sylvan redoubled his work for conservation. "He threw himself into his work," Ramon noted.

Sylvan's love for music also helped him to deal with the loneliness. He'd play the piano for hours, sometimes pounding out songs at night when he couldn't sleep. He often entertained fellow patrons at bars or restaurants with honky-tonk tunes. "Piano-playing was part of who he was," Ramon said.

Ramon, who was about to enter college when his mother died, agonized not only over her death, but also over his obligation to stay and help his father. Sylvan thought first of his son, however, urging Ramon to go to school and continue his education.

"You're really kind of ready to step into adult life, and you need to get to doing that," Ramon remembers his father saying. "He gave me a push, which was very important," Ramon acknowledged. "He was anxious for me to continue to discover who I was. I think that defined who he was to me in a very positive way," Ramon said. "It was a bad situation, but he'd faced bad situations before, and he'd roll up his sleeves and work through them."

Sylvan strove to be a good parent for Karen, Marilyn, and Ramon. Half a century later Karen, now Prasannata, recalled those childhood days and how she idolized her father. "I loved his involvement with the woods," she said. "He talked to me a lot about his work and I really knew he loved it." With a father who preached soil fertility, no wonder that some of Karen's first words were "phosphorous" and "potash." She was delighted when she could tag along to watch as Sylvan taught farmers how to lay out contour strips in their fields.

Sylvan about 1950.

Karen so admired Sylvan that she often imitated him, right down to his stiff-legged gait from the war injury. Occasionally Sylvan would take her along to his office, where she might draw pictures on a blackboard. If she had to stay home with a neighbor who cared for her, she grew restless and longed to be with her father.

One day the 6-year-old girl hatched a plan to meet her dad after work. With her dog, a "great buddy" Labrador mix named George, Karen slipped away from her baby-sitter and started off through Ottumwa's evening rush-hour traffic. When she stumbled and skinned her knee in the middle of a busy street, George pulled her to safety at the curb. Karen stood there crying until a man and woman stopped to help. They took her to the police station, where Karen told authorities she was on her way to see her father.

The call from the police surprised Sylvan, who had no reason to suspect that his daughter was a "runaway." Sylvan eventually found Karen devouring a hamburger, french fries, and chocolate malt with a police escort at the nearby Pantry café. "Oh, we're glad to see you," Sylvan said, as he gave Karen a hug and took her home.

Bernie Neff met Sylvan in 1951. She loved his zest for life, which included flying to lunch dates in a rented plane.

Prasannata still marvels at her father's ability to deal with his children. He could not punish his little adventurer's independence and love for her dad. Rather, he acknowledged her free spirit and demonstrated the calm, even temperament his family came to cherish.

That was just one of the qualities that caught the attention of a young home economist and Iowa State College graduate whom Sylvan met May 12, 1951. They spoke briefly while they were watching the Veishea parade on a sunny Saturday at the Iowa State campus in Ames. "Meet Bernadine Neff — watching parade," read a short entry in his diary. He waited several months before he called "Bernie" to ask for a date. She accepted, igniting a love affair that was to last 43 years.

The fact that Bernie lived in Muscatine and Sylvan lived in Ottumwa was only a minor obstacle to the romance. Sylvan sometimes would take a long noon hour and fly a rented plane to Muscatine to pick

up Bernie. The couple then would fly to Moline for lunch at a cafe across from the airport. Bernie treasured Sylvan's passion for life and his gentle nature. And she soon gave him the nickname "Sy." They were married in December 1952. Bernie's love, support, and companionship helped him to start a new chapter in his life.

After a one-year courtship, Sylvan married Bernie Neff on December 15, 1952.

CHAPTER 10

THE BIOLOGIST

"HE WAS OUR ENVIRONMENTAL ETHIC, OUR ENVIRONMENTAL CONSCIENCE."

Back at work for the Soil Conservation Service in the agency's Ottumwa office, Sylvan quickly developed a reputation as a dedicated employee and outdoorsman. As a district conservationist, his duties included designing farm conservation plans, leading workshops for farmers, speaking to school groups, and promoting wildlife habitat. His SCS associates, as well as the public he served, knew "Runk" as an amicable, sometimes eccentric character.

"You couldn't find him or his desk for the pile of books," recalled Paul Ohland, who also worked in the Ottumwa field office. But Sylvan generally knew where to look for important papers in his avalanche of "file piles."

After treks to farm ponds to sample the fish populations, Sylvan might hang his wet nets in the office window to dry. He raised salamander tadpoles or other critters in an aquarium on his desk. When

As a biologist for the U. S. Soil Conservation Service, Sylvan regularly was called upon to identify fungi, flowers, or wild animals.

he found a snake on a field trip, he'd often tuck it into his shirt or jacket. He never tired of teasing his companions by trying to shake their hands with a snake protruding from his sleeve.

A forester at heart and by training, Sylvan did not let his leg injury keep him from working in the woods when he came back to the U. S. Soil Conservation Service after World War II.

Sylvan made sure the practical joke stopped short of harm to the snake, however. Coworker John Worster recalled Sylvan's concern for a hognose snake he'd brought into the office. Sylvan carefully returned the creature to the site where he'd found it, all the while worrying that a predator might catch it.

As he studied soil conservation on farms, Sylvan realized that the traditional emphasis on crop fields often neglected wildlife habitat and woodlands. He urged farmers and SCS farm planners to consider wildlife as an integral part of each farm conservation plan.

In 1953 he was appointed to a new position: soil conservationist. It's tempting to assume that Sylvan wrote his own ticket. The job description included plant studies, wildlife habitat planning and management, and work with other agencies to promote wildlife. Sylvan also helped to put on fishing clinics and sometimes staffed SCS booths at county fairs and sports shows.

Sylvan foresaw the need to manage the thousands of farm ponds that were being built in southern Iowa in the 1950s. He urged more work on strip mine reclamation and revegetation. He noted the rapid conversion of forests to pasture or cropland and called for a set of criteria to determine when the practice was justified.

At first, Sylvan worked mostly in southern Iowa and lived with his family in Ottumwa. In 1958 his office was transferred to Des Moines, although he and Bernie kept their home in Ottumwa. He sometimes rode the bus to Des Moines on Monday, then waited for Bernie to come get him on Friday night. The whole family moved to Des Moines in 1961.

By 1962 Sylvan had proposed a further expansion of his assignments and another new title: biologist. The job carried with it the responsibility to assist farmers, SCS staff, sportsmen's groups, and other organizations with a host of wildlife and woodlands issues. Sylvan regularly conducted field training and demonstrations for SCS employees. He held countless meetings with wildlife and forestry colleagues from Iowa State University and the Iowa Conservation Commission. Sylvan attended up to 15 or 20 night meetings per month with farmers or conservation groups. Because of his long and irregular hours, Sylvan persuaded SCS officials to issue him his own key to the Federal Building in downtown Des Moines.

Sylvan wrote papers on wildlife conservation and sometimes taught short courses on such diverse topics as using black plastic to kill pond weeds, the benefits of fencerows for wildlife, and how to manage habitat for cottontail rabbits. Other SCS colleagues sent him wildflowers, tree leaves, berries, mushrooms — even snapping turtle eggs — to identify.

Sylvan and his boss, the late Frank Mendell, agreed on the need for conservation education. Mendell gave Sylvan free rein to present public programs and lead nature hikes. Sylvan received dozens of requests to speak as his reputation as a naturalist spread across the state. Despite the busy travel schedule, he welcomed the chance to meet more people and to help them "get acquainted" with their environment.

Sylvan's respect for things natural, along with his sense of humor and easygoing manner, made him a good spokesman for conservation. As an SCS worker, he talked individually with thousands of landowners, explaining the benefits of soil, water, and wildlife conservation to their farms, said Carl Zimmerman, district conservationist in Adams County from 1943 to 1971.

Part of the secret, said Sylvan's longtime secretary, Wilma Kimball, was that "he could talk anybody's language." Whether dealing with a teacher, farmer, or administrator, Sylvan might tell jokes, trade stories, drink coffee — and eventually gain another convert to the conservation cause. "It just rubbed off," Kimball said.

There was no badgering or criticism of landowners, Kimball said, but it was hard to resist Sylvan's sincere, subtle plea to respect the "fellow citizens" — plant and animal — with which we share our community. "We really can't manage land properly in a long time sense unless we do recognize what Nature is doing," Sylvan said.

Even fellow SCS employees, who sometimes grew tired of agency training sessions, looked forward to field days with Sylvan. "I learned that a walk down a road ditch could be a memorable experience," marveled one worker.

Unlike some bureaucrats, Sylvan offered practical ideas that would fit in on a working farm, noted Roger Koster, a former district and area conservationist for the SCS in Clayton and nearby counties. "He could relate to any farmer. He was like a comfortable old shoe — very serviceable," Koster said.

"He made you feel important," Koster added. "You were his equal in his eyes. The farmer didn't even realize he was being trained. He thought it was conversation. But it stuck with him. His training was a fun learning experience," Koster said.

In a wetland Sylvan would offer tastes of arrowhead and cattail tubers, then joke about how Native Americans and pioneers survived on the muddy-tasting food. With a twinkle in his eye, Sylvan would ponder the merits of ginseng, which folklore says is a sexual tonic. He'd show how to string a wire to persuade birds to plant their own habitat. As they sat on the perch, the birds would deposit undigested seeds, complete with a dose of fertilizer, in their droppings.

Nature abounds with these "contracts," Sylvan said. He demonstrated how the itch of stinging nettles could be soothed with the juice from jewelweed, which often grows near the nettles. When quizzed about the value of poison ivy, Sylvan noted how people learn to avoid the pesky plant — and therefore give more space to fragile species growing in the area.

Sylvan advocated wise use of Earth's resources, while pointing out how abuse of the land can upset the balance of a natural community. For instance, cattle grazing in a woodland destroy the trees just as effectively as a bulldozer, he said. It just takes the animals a little longer to eat the seedlings, compact the soil, and reduce the trees' resistance to insects and disease.

To Sylvan there was no such thing as "waste" land, said Bart McAninch, another SCS coworker. "He was the champion of non-cropland," McAninch said. "It was like he was defending a minority or an unpopular cause. Every acre is being used and contributing to the community," said McAninch, repeating Sylvan's mantra.

The teaching and storytelling continued at mealtime, which Sylvan often shared with families of farmers or coworkers when he was traveling. McAninch said his young sons anticipated such visits and Sylvan's outdoor tales, which were "better than any movie." Sylvan's SCS friends teased him about his stories, wondering whether the next tale would be a five-acre story or a 10-acre story. And you'd better be sitting down if he decided to spin a 40-acre yarn.

An avid duck hunter, Sylvan posed with mallards he bagged on opening day in 1955.

His associates looked forward to Sylvan's wild-food dinners. After a successful fall hunt, he hosted the Ottumwa SCS office staff for a meal of wild duck, wild rice, and mushrooms. Following the meal, he unveiled photos of the mushrooms, along with pictures of a similar, poisonous fungus. "I think I got the right one . . .," he mused.

At a 1964 dinner for their friends Phil and Veda Babcock, Sylvan and Bernie served wild leek soup, evening primrose roots, spring beauty bulbs, creamed milkweed on toast, steamed nettles, morel mushrooms, and cattail shoots. "Maybe it's the Indian in me," Sylvan told WHO radio reporter Lee Kline during an interview at the feast. "If you can see a plant that you know is good to eat and you know a little what it tastes like, it adds another dimension to the enjoyment of your trip through the woods."

A fellow biologist recalled riding past a northwest Iowa marsh when Sylvan suddenly shouted, "Stop the car! The cattails are blooming!" The two men got out and gathered a bag of cattail pollen for Sylvan to add to his next morning's pancake batter.

Bernie helped her husband to introduce friends to wild edibles. "We made an agreement a long time ago that anything he would bring home and clean, I would cook," Bernie said. "I didn't say I'd eat it — I just would cook it!"

Sylvan got to do the cooking in 1967 when Des Moines hosted the national Soil and Water Conservation Society of America convention. He was charged with supervising a pit barbecue and preparing truckloads of sweet corn for the visitors. Sons Tom and Jon still groan about picking sweet corn. Bernie arranged the spouses' activities, including a tour of the Amana Colonies.

His sense of humor endeared Sylvan to SCS workers across the state. At an awards banquet, Sylvan praised the dedication of his colleagues. "They are so enthusiastic about saving soil that they refuse to clean their fingernails," he teased. "Even their bathtubs have contour lines around them — inside that is!"

Agronomist John Maddy, who shared an office with Sylvan, found a way to poke fun back at his friend. On an outing with Maddy, Sylvan found a rare plant, which he marked in preparation for a field trip the next day. But Maddy tipped off the group before the tour. When Sylvan pointed to the plant, expecting no one to know what it was, the men shouted its name. Sylvan was astonished — until he realized that Maddy had spilled the beans.

John Botts of Albia recalled an SCS dinner when Sylvan was seated by an unnamed "big shot," who was studying his notes for a speech. "Runk hoisted his stiff leg up on the table and lit a cigar and said it was 'a bunch of bull' — and then he lit the notes on fire," Botts chuckled. The crowd howled with delight at the antics of Sylvan and his "big shot" co-conspirator, who accomplished their mission of bringing a bit of levity to a routine meeting.

In days before political correctness, Sylvan occasionally spiced up his conservation slide talks by slipping in a picture of topless women from the South Sea Islands. He'd feign surprise when the image popped up between a picture of a contoured field and a farm pond.

Sylvan's sense of humor may have helped to divert attention from his other habits. Promptness, for example, was not one of his strong suits. Memos sometimes lay buried on Sylvan's desk for weeks. "Don't you ever answer your mail?" wrote one exasperated colleague.

Yet, Sylvan seemed to make time to help youths and to spread the conservation education message. When a Utah schoolboy sent a one-sentence "Dear Sirs" letter asking about uses for farm waste materials, Sylvan composed a full-page response about corn, soybean, and forest products, and suggested additional sources. Here was a young person who deserved an answer that might lead him to get better acquainted with his community — and Sylvan did not want to miss the "teachable moment."

That was typical Sylvan Runkel, said his secretary. He was ready to help anyone who asked, whether the question was about identifying a plant or dealing with the bureaucracy. "He was the authority," Kimball said.

In 1959 Sylvan received a commendation from the Iowa Farm Safety Council for identifying and providing information about poisonous pokeberries, horse nettle berries, and buckeyes that several children had eaten in three separate incidents. In each case doctors pumped the stomachs of the youngsters. The physicians said that Sylvan's quick assessment of the situations may have saved the children's lives.

He also earned the Iowa "Civil Servant of the Year" award in 1965. An SCS "Special Achievement Award" in 1972 cited his conservation education work.

Sylvan would be the first to admit that he made some mistakes, however. During his CCC days, for example, he advocated planting black locust seedlings for erosion control and reforestation. The thorny trees later became pests as they invaded pastures and woodlands.

Sylvan often made aerial photos of SCS projects and conservation problems or techniques. The SCS used many of those photos in their publications. He photographed this example of contour farming and strip cropping near Creston, Iowa.

In the 1950s and 1960s the SCS and the Iowa Conservation Commission recommended planting multiflora rose, autumn olive, and honeysuckle for wildlife habitat. Sylvan joined the bandwagon to promote the shrubs. Within a few years multiflora rose became a major pest, especially in southern Iowa. Autumn olive and honeysuckle also are now considered undesirable, invasive species.

Sylvan and others also suggested seeding bromegrass to control erosion along roadsides and in sloping fields. Ironically, brome now is a serious weed problem in native and reconstructed prairies that Sylvan tried to protect.

But Sylvan also had the vision to criticize heavy use of insecticides, even before the landmark publication of Rachel Carson's *Silent Spring* in 1962. As early as 1958 Sylvan had begun raising questions about SCS policies espousing pesticide use. In 1960 he prepared a reference suggesting natural alternatives to chemical insecticides. Overuse of chemicals was like "burning down the barn to get rid of a few rats," Sylvan observed.

In the early 1950s, as the U. S. Army Corps of Engineers was planning the Red Rock, Saylorville, Coralville, and Rathbun reservoirs, Sylvan and other conservationists warned that the pools would silt in rapidly without better conservation practices in the watersheds. Today's mudflats at upper ends of all four reservoirs validate those predictions.

Even though he was a forester, Sylvan had to admit that trees aren't appropriate for some sites. In 1962 he wrote a critique of a U. S. Forest Service plan to promote more tree-planting and woodland management in western Iowa. While Sylvan dutifully praised the study for helping to provide information about the region, he pointed out that the area — which now has gained prominence as "the Loess Hills" — was not particularly well suited to growing trees. Sylvan urged state and federal officials to conduct more soil surveys, woodland suitability studies, and landowner education before launching a major tree-planting effort. In later years he advocated clearing trees that encroached on the Loess Hills prairies.

Sylvan grew increasingly skeptical of practices that seemed likely to jeopardize the web that holds natural communities together. By the first Earth Day, April 22, 1970, he was becoming more comfortable with the term "environmentalist," said his son Tom. "I think he evolved, too. Maybe the times caught up with him." At age 63, Sylvan empathized with high school and college students who led Earth Day demonstrations demanding better protection of our environment.

Indeed, for several years Sylvan had been prodding his superiors to ensure that SCS policies protected wildlife habitat and sustainable land use. He served on a committee to study how to repair damage caused by SCS waterway projects and by county road construction. His associates

Other SCS employees looked forward to learning about "natural citizens" in lively training sessions with Sylvan. (SCS PHOTO BY LYNN BETTS)

claimed that Sylvan's determination helped to end an SCS policy that promoted stream channelization. Sylvan argued that such stream straightening and clearing along the banks destroyed habitat. "He was our environmental ethic, our environmental conscience," declared Eldon Weber, an SCS colleague.

"He didn't mind saying what he thought" as he pushed the agency do more for the environment, said another SCS friend. "The so-called hierarchy of the service didn't faze him one bit," said John Botts, who worked with Sylvan in Monroe County about 1950. "He was one of those unflappable guys."

To Sylvan, conservation was not just a job, but rather a responsibility toward the "web of life" that people share with wildflowers and wildlife. "He was dedicated," said Kimball. "That was his whole life."

Still, Sylvan found time for fun, Kimball said. He frequently went to work early so he could leave early for one of his children's school functions or other activities. Faced with the government's bare-bones telephone system, Sylvan and a coworker took matters into their own hands and rigged up wires to give all the office mates their own phones. "You couldn't have had a better place to work," Kimball said. "He treated everybody with respect" — from fellow employees to farmers to the general public, she said.

Sylvan also could be a peacemaker, if necessary, she noted. "If you got in a mess, Sylvan would help you figure it out." Sylvan's likeable personality also brought out the best in his fellow employees, Kimball said. "He could talk you into doing anything!"

With Sylvan as piano player, fellow SCS employees formed a band to play at the agency's social gatherings in the 1960s. Others in the band are (from left) John Maddy, Doug Melton, Bill Ludwig and Harry Darling.

One of Kimball's favorite memories of Sylvan was his musical talent. He and four SCS friends formed a dance band dubbed "The Picker-Shellers," later renamed the "The SCS Combine." They were a big hit at many SCS parties in the 1950s and '60s. "He could really pound that piano," Kimball said. "He'd have that one leg sticking out there…"

At an SCS Christmas party the "clunker of a piano" couldn't handle Sylvan's lively music, Kimball recalled. The keys started popping off during his jam session, but Sylvan remained nonchalant. "He just kept on going, with the ivories just flying," she laughed.

Sylvan performed his job with the same enthusiasm, suggested Bart McAninch. He was on a mission to make conservation fun and to bring it to the people.

"To me, he was the Aldo Leopold of our time," McAninch declared. "He was the ultimate conservationist with a special phrase that made any concept seem simple and easy to understand. He made it seem so real."

CHAPTER 11

THE NEW FAMILY

"HE GAVE RESPECT."

After their 1952 marriage, Sy and Bernie often spent evenings at the Ottumwa American Legion club, where they could eat, dance, or visit with friends. Knowing Sy's reputation as a spirited pianist, the other patrons often enticed him to play their favorite tunes.

Then the family began to grow and the couple's focus turned to their children. Their first child, Tom, was born in October 1953. Jon followed in 1955, while Jeff was born in 1958. With the three boys and their older half-sister, Karen, the Runkel home became a lively place.

Although Bernie had been a home economist in Muscatine and Clinton counties, she quit her job when she married, as did most young women in that era. During the 1950s and 1960s she served as homemaker and full-time mother for Karen, Tom, Jon, and Jeff.

Bernie usually shared Sy's interest in the outdoors. She cringed, though, when he caught garter snakes for their infant sons to touch. And when Sy brought home a snapping turtle, it was banished to the garage. By the time Jeff acquired his pet lizard, "Stanley Thaddeus," Bernie had grown somewhat more accustomed to having critters for houseguests.

As the boys grew older they clamored for a chance to go with Sy when he traveled on SCS business in Iowa. "We got to see a lot of neat places," Tom recalled. "But we wouldn't go too far before he'd have to stop

Bernie with Karen, Tom, and Jon at the family's Ottumwa home in the mid-1950s.

and look somebody up," Jon added. "He knew a lot of people."

When Tom was about 5, he hid in the car when Sy drove to the Ottumwa airport to fly over a farm conservation project. While Bernie was frantically searching around their home for the youngster, Sy called to say he'd found Tom. The boy got an airplane ride, along with a scolding.

When Sy was at home, he firmly but quietly handled most of the family discipline. "You knew a rule was a rule," said Bernie. The boys realized they were in trouble if Sy said, "Let's go in the den." But the punishment usually consisted of a lecture and a swat on the behind, followed by a warm hug.

"He never tried to put anybody down," Bernie said. "You did something you shouldn't have done — but you're not a bad girl or bad boy," she said, reiterating Sy's child-rearing advice.

"He had an uncanny ability to get the best out of you," added Jeff. "You wanted to do good. If you were doing something goofy, he wouldn't be yelling at you." Instead, Sy would say something like, "You might want to re-think what would be the best thing to do here," Jeff said.

"It wasn't yellin' and screamin'," Jeff said. "He could hurt you more with a look. It worked pretty well."

Even as a teenager, Jon admired his father. "I never had anything but respect for him," Jon said. "But he also gave respect. He just wouldn't ever have anything negative to say."

Sy's sense of right and wrong impressed those around him. Jeff recalled a gathering where a man was boasting about all the catfish he'd caught, even though he didn't have a fishing license. Sy listened quietly, then approached the acquaintance with another perspective on fishing licenses. "You know, the idea isn't to cheat the state out of a few fish. The idea is to pay for conservation," Sy said.

"He wasn't trying to put him down in front of people or anything," Jeff said. "He was mentoring." Thereafter, the sheepish man dutifully bought his license.

After several years of Sy's living in Ottumwa but working in the Des Moines office, the whole family moved to the capital city on January 20, 1961. It was a bitter-cold day when the nation watched John F. Kennedy's inaugural and heard his famous words: "Ask not what your country can do for you. Ask what you can do for your country."

The Runkels had to go to the neighbor's to see the speech, however. The family still did not have a TV set — and neither Sy nor Bernie was in any hurry to buy one. Sy longed for the days when people sat and talked, bringing young and old closer together. "It may be that this [TV and radio] has caused much of the breakdown in family communication!" he later wrote to a grandson. The couple finally relented and bought a TV set about 1963. Their sons were sure they would be the last family in Des Moines to own a television.

The three Runkel boys sometimes made their own entertainment by playing soldier. They often mimicked their father's way of walking with his stiff knee. Despite his traumatic military experience, Sy did not discourage his sons' war games, which were typical of grade school boys in the '60s. One of the family's Christmas cards showed Tom, Jon, and Jeff in their toy army helmets. When their friends noticed Sy's straight leg, the Runkel children boasted about their father's heroism and how he'd survived the war. Sy tried not to bring attention to his other injuries, however. Jon was in high school before he realized the extent of the dental work his father had needed to repair the damage from the D-Day crash.

Sy's knowledge of the natural world not only served him well in his SCS job, but also helped in dealing with the antics of his kids. When Karen burned her fingers on a hot grill at an office cookout, Sy immediately plunged her hand into a pitcher of iced tea. He explained to the startled picnickers that the tannic acid would help to relieve the pain.

Once, when Sy was not home, Jeff mischievously persuaded a

In the early 1960s sons Jon, Tom, and Jeff (left to right) donned toy army helmets and uniforms and sometimes walked stiff-legged to emulate their father's military career.

neighbor boy to eat some mushrooms, insisting that they were marshmallows. The playmate's mother was panic-stricken. She rushed the child to the hospital to have his stomach pumped. When Sy returned, he assured the family that the fungi were not poisonous. But his advice was too late to save the boy from an ordeal.

The Runkel boys found their dad a valuable resource when they studied history, Jon said. "It was almost like talking to a living encyclopedia." Sy could tell stories about his memories of historic events: the November 11, 1918, armistice that ended World War I; Charles Lindbergh's solo flight across the Atlantic in 1927; the explosion of the dirigible Hindenburg, in 1937; the Armistice Day blizzard of November 11, 1940, which killed many duck hunters; the December 7, 1941, attack at Pearl Harbor that dragged the United States into World War II; and, of course, the June 6, 1944, D-Day invasion in which Sy nearly died.

His sons Jeff, Jon, and Tom shared Sylvan's passion for hunting. Sylvan photographed them and the family dog, Wiesie, after a successful hunt in 1967.

Sy tried to spend time outdoors with his children whenever he could. Often they'd go fishing for bluegills in the pond of a farmer Sy had met through his SCS work. On trips to the family cabin on Trout Lake, Minnesota, they'd fish all morning, take a lunch break, then fish until dark.

One summer afternoon, however, Sy unexpectedly came home from work and began playing with his sons. Bernie immediately realized that something was bothering him. He confided later that he had just come from a farm pond where two children had drowned.

Guns and shooting were a normal part of the Runkel household. Sy took the family to trapshoots at the Ottumwa Izaak Walton League, and he couldn't wait until his sons were big enough to go hunting. Bernie recalls sitting in a boat with a toddler in her arms, waiting for Sy to stalk ducks in a marsh. When the boys grew older, the whole family joined Sy on duck and pheasant hunts. At first only Sy would carry a gun — his father's classic Model 12 Winchester 12-gauge shotgun. Bernie laughed that she was the "bird dog," while Karen, Tom, Jon, and Jeff would carry toy guns or binoculars.

Tom still amazes his friends with the tale of a cock pheasant that flushed beneath his feet, caught his binocular strap, and flew away with the plastic binoculars dangling from the bird's neck. The farmer found pieces of the binoculars as he plowed the cornfield the next spring.

When the boys reached adolescence, Sy took them on real hunting trips. They seldom missed an opening day of duck or pheasant season. But Sy often reminded his sons that hunting also meant respect for the resource, Jon said.

"If you shot it, you ate it," Bernie declared. "We brought it home and cleaned it." Jeff still grimaces at the taste of the coot he shot — and had to eat. "Never again!" he chuckled.

His sons sometimes grew impatient with their father's penchant for teaching, however. "Even out duck hunting, he'd have to stop and point something out," Tom said. "A lot of times, we'd say, 'Let's get going! I don't want to hear about another plant right now!'"

In retrospect, the boys realized that their 60-something father probably needed a rest from trying to keep up with his teenage sons, and that he probably had some good information to share. "It makes me feel a little guilty that I didn't pay more attention," said Jeff.

Sy didn't take up deer hunting until he was in his 60s, but he continued it until he was in his 80s. He enjoyed the outing and the camaraderie. Jon chuckled about a hunt when Sy dropped a deer with one shot. "Right between the eyes," shouted Jon, as they approached the fallen animal. "It wasn't bad," agreed Sy, "considering I was aiming at the heart."

He taught his sons the Native American belief that hunters must show respect, even reverence, for the game on which their lives depended. Sy also told of the German tradition of putting a twig in the mouth of a freshly killed deer to give the animal its "last bite." "I still say a little prayer" after killing an animal, Jeff said.

Sy's passion for hunting and fishing was tied to his delight in observing the world around him, Tom said. "Father was connected. That was his life, basically. He was one of the lucky few people who got to work in something he actually loved," Tom said. "His profession was his hobby."

Although Sy's leg limited his ability to play baseball or other sports with his children, he found other innovative types of recreation. He amazed the youngsters with his ability to ride a bicycle backward, sitting on the handlebars and facing to the rear while pedaling.

After a fresh snow or ice storm, Sy and the boys might take the family car to a large parking lot where they'd spin "doughnuts" on the slick pavement. His sons still marvel at Sy's ability to smoothly shift a standard transmission car with his stiff leg.

Sy liked to tell stories about his father's motorcycles and his own motorcycle-riding days. "You don't really know what a mountain is like until you've ridden down it on a motorcycle," he said, hinting at some hair-raising trips on a two-wheeler.

When Jon began to tinker with cars and motorcycles, Sy took the hands-off approach. He offered mechanical advice, but he let his son do the work. He owned very few tools, and seldom used the ones he had.

In the early 1970s, when Tom and Jon wanted to ride their motorcycles off the road, Sy allowed them to go on trails that were soon to be flooded by the Saylorville Reservoir along the Des Moines River north of Des Moines. "Boys have to have a little excitement," he shrugged, when Bernie worried about the dangers of the sport. But Sy forbade his sons from riding on illicit trails at Brown's Woods, a natural area that the Polk County Conservation Board eventually protected. Sy spoke in favor of the project and led hikes to Brown's Woods to promote its preservation.

Music remained a significant part of Sy's life. Besides performing on the piano in a band with his SCS colleagues, he regularly played at Cub Scout pack meetings, both with Ramon in the 1930s and for his younger sons in the 1960s. Sy also composed songs for family members or special events. Bernie is partial to "Bernadine from Ol' Muscatine." But the most famous composition is Sy's "Ode to the Loess Hills," which he wrote in the 1980s for the Loess Hills Prairie Seminar. For two decades participants at the annual event have sung the Ode "with exuberance and gusto," as Sylvan instructed in his scribbled note on the original musical score.

Jon and several grandchildren also shared Sy's love for music and talent on the piano. For a time, the Runkels had two pianos, one regular and one miniature, where Jon and Sy played duets.

The family calendar nearly always was filled with Boy Scout and conservation group meetings, along with Sylvan's many speaking engagements and nature hikes. As much as Sylvan traveled for both work and pleasure, he refused to let Iowa winters interfere with his plans. "You never stayed home from anything because of the weather," Bernie said.

Bernie and the whole family sometimes went along on Sy's business conferences and field trips as part of their vacation. The Runkels traveled to a 1965 Soil Conservation Society of America meeting in Jackson, Mississippi, then went on to Florida. While in the Sunshine State, Sy celebrated his 59th birthday by proving that he could water ski with a stiff leg.

Another family vacation centered on the Soil and Water Conservation Society of America convention in Albuquerque, New Mexico, in 1966. Side trips included the Black Hills, Mount Rushmore, Colorado, the Philmont Scout Ranch, and a short backpacking jaunt in the Four Corners area.

In 1964 the family drove to New York City to the World's Fair. They stopped at other attractions, such as the Statue of Liberty, Gettysburg, Pennsylvania, and Niagara Falls. "If there was a place to go, we'd go," Bernie said. The family visited museums in Chicago, a Cardinals baseball game in St. Louis, and "Minnesota at the drop of a hat," Bernie said.

The Runkels nearly always had a canine pet, although Sy purported not to like dogs. (He teased Bernie by saying he wouldn't take a bath if she bathed a dog in the tub.) George, a Labrador mix, endeared himself to Sy when the dog rescued Karen after she'd fallen on a busy Ottumwa street.

Later, when George strayed away from Sy and Bernie while they were boating near their cabin at Trout Lake, the family was heartbroken. When several fishermen found and returned the dog several days later, Sy spontaneously picked up George and hugged him.

Perhaps Sy envied George's fishing skills. On one Trout Lake fishing trip George watched curiously as Sy and other anglers in the boat hooked several walleyes but failed to land the splashing fish. Finally, when Sy caught another fish, George leapt into the water, grabbed the walleye in his mouth, and swam back to the boat with the prize.

As George's health failed, the family bought another dog. Sylvan named the purebred black Labrador "Wiesenboden," the German term for a rich, black, swampy soil. The friendly male dog became "Wiesie" for short.

When Wiese died of an infection while Jeff was in high school, the family soon got another male Lab, and named it Wiesie II.

Wiezie, a female black Labrador that Sylvan and Bernie adopted in the early 1980s.

Jeff, Sylvan, Bernie, Jon, and Tom celebrate Jon's and Jeff's Eagle Scout awards in 1973.

Sylvan's final Lab, which he and Bernie got in the 1980s, was a female, so the couple changed the spelling to Wiezie.

After Wiezie died in 1999, Bernie bought the fourth black Lab, which she named "Ivy," or "IV," for number four.

As much as he loved the mountains and wild places, why did Sy spend most of his life in Iowa, with a family, pets, a government job, and a home in the city? Son Jeff, who now lives in Montana, sometimes discussed the question with his dad.

"It felt right," Jeff said. "He always felt this was his home...a feeling he was belonging to an area, to the land. I think he really liked the aspect of the prairie," he continued. "And also the timber. And growing up on the Mississippi. He could find diversity," Jeff noted. "And the people had a lot to do with it." Sy genuinely enjoyed working with farmers and other Iowans.

"I think he just loved the place," Jeff concluded. "It probably has something to do with that spiritual thing. It's just a feeling you get about the place. There's just no place on Earth you'd rather be."

CHAPTER 12

SCOUTS

"THE SCOUT... BECOMES A PART OF THE GREAT NATURAL AGE-OLD SYSTEM."

Searching for fun and excitement, 12-year-old Sylvan Runkel joined Boy Scout Troop 6 in Moline in 1918. Members of the fledgling organization had no uniforms, but Sylvan and his friends looked forward to Monday night meetings at the McKinley Grade School gymnasium. The loose-knit troop especially relished outdoor adventures, such as their frequent outings into the woods and hills around Moline.

Sylvan couldn't have known then what a profound influence the Boy Scouts would have on shaping his life. More than 60 years later, at a Boy Scout Sunday church service in Des Moines, he reminisced about those early days of Scouting.

Sylvan shared his love of the West and the high country by leading Boy Scouts on wilderness trips. He's shown here with Scouts on Mount Baldy, a 12,441-foot peak on the Philmont Scout Ranch in New Mexico. (PHOTO BY SHAWN DAVIS)

"I became imprinted with such things as hiking, camping, campfire cookery, nature study... and a general love and respect for all of the great and wild natural outdoors," Sylvan recalled. "The Scout develops a feeling of kinship with the natural communities of woodlands, rivers, hills, and prairies. He gets a feeling of belonging to this great natural world — he becomes a part of the great natural age-old system."

Sylvan's sister Geneva said his Moline Scoutmaster, Rudy Bracker, served as a role model for Sylvan and coached him in outdoor skills. Bracker took the boys on hikes and campouts, and he was instrumental in founding Camp Mansur, along the Green River east of Moline, where the Scouts spent a week each summer. The camp and the Scout programs reinforced Sylvan's love of camping, woodcraft, and nature study.

Even when he reached age 18, too old for regular Scouting, Sylvan stayed with the troop as an assistant Scoutmaster. "Scouting was very important to him — the honorableness of it," said Geneva.

His early experiences convinced Sylvan that Scouting helped to build character and honor in young men and broadened their horizons as they

Sylvan and his son Jeff donned their backpacks and Scout uniforms as they prepared to depart on a trip to Philmont Scout Ranch, New Mexico, in 1972.

moved into adulthood. "I believe this has no equal in helping a boy build a foundation for his life," he said.

"To see life as a great adventure — and to find and grasp its opportunities — demands guidance," Sylvan told the Scout Sunday congregation. He felt strongly that some of the best guidance outside the home comes from groups like Boy Scouts. He had been working with Scouts on tree-planting and other conservation service projects since his CCC days in the 1930s.

Sylvan also saw the results in his own sons, whom he encouraged to join Cub Scouts and Boy Scouts. He must have been bursting with pride in November 1947 when son Ramon earned his Eagle Scout rank — the highest in Scouting. Because Sylvan had advanced only as far as the First Class badge, he especially appreciated the dedication that had gone into Ray's award, and he'd pushed his son to reach that goal.

After Ray completed his Scouting career, and before his younger sons became Scouts, Sylvan served as a counselor, helping Ottumwa youths with nature, conservation, or forestry merit badges. He became even more active in the 1960s when sons Tom, Jon, and Jeff became old enough to join Troop 201 at Glen Echo Christian Church in Des Moines. All three earned the Eagle rank. Later, to Sylvan's great pleasure, four of his grandsons became Eagle Scouts. They were Ramon's sons, Tim and Nathan; Tom's son, Ted; and Marilyn's son, Anthony.

Of his many Scouting activities, Sylvan especially loved the Philmont Scout Ranch in New Mexico, which he first visited in 1969 at age 62. The 138,000-acre site is a high adventure base where Scouts from all over the world can get a taste of wilderness. "On those clear, cold nights in the high country at Philmont, those stars seem so close," Sylvan sighed.

Despite the difficulties of hiking in the mountainous backcountry with his stiff leg, Sylvan returned twice more. He became an inspiration to some of the young Scouts who struggled to make the rigorous trek. Although he was just 15 when he accompanied Sylvan on the 1975 trip to Philmont, Steve Davis of Des Moines said the experience remains etched in his mind.

"He had this big old canvas pack with a metal frame, and he had his camera around his neck and a chair that he hung on the back that dangled down. And he had the Sierra cup," Davis recalled, describing the metal cup with a wire handle that hung on Sylvan's belt. "We all had to get Sierra cups, because Sylvan had a Sierra cup." The boys idolized Sylvan.

Even with his stiff leg and cane, Sylvan was not deterred from taking wilderness trips with Boy Scouts, and hiking the same trails that they did — like this precarious stream crossing in Wyoming's Bridger Wilderness.

"This guy isn't some eccentric little old man, he's this really interesting guy that all of us fantasize about. He's done it," Davis marveled. He recalled the nights when Sylvan mesmerized the Scouts with stories around the campfire.

"When you're a 15-year-old kid, you're not really thinking about plants and a lot of nature. But when a guy has stories about plane crashes during the war and grizzly bears and throwing an ax and forest fires and all these just spellbinding stories, and he tells you that this planet is significant and he takes time to admire it and tell you about it, it is significant.

"In my scrapbook, I have a lot of pictures of plants, of all things, at a time when I wasn't particularly interested in wildflowers," Davis said. Although he and the other Scouts may not have been avid botanists, they still took note and remembered when Sylvan stopped to point out an interesting flower. The boys were amazed at his knowledge of plant life, and they often tried to find plants that he couldn't identify. "But you couldn't stump Sy!" Davis laughed.

Sylvan also showed the boys camping basics: how to keep their food safe from bears and mice and weather, and how to start a fire in the rain. "He just had a gentle way of telling us what we needed to know," Davis said. Sylvan let the Scouts do most of the fire-building, cooking, and other camp chores. But he occasionally added his own touch — such as cooking nettles for greens, or picking wild onions to spice up bland, dehydrated spaghetti sauce.

Another former Scout, Brad Davis of Des Moines, joined Sylvan on a 1976 wilderness trip to Wyoming's Summit Lake, where Sylvan had camped nearly 40 years before. "I can remember him standing there and just looking out," Davis said. Sylvan obviously welcomed the chance to return to the site and to share its beauty with another generation of wilderness-lovers. Perhaps Sylvan also was recalling the bison skull he'd found along the trail four decades earlier.

Brad Davis called his leader "Mr. Outdoorsman of Iowa." "He was the ultimate Scout. It was just fascinating to me that somebody would know all that stuff," Davis continued. He compared Sylvan to the legendary mountain man Jim Bridger. "When you were with him, you felt you were with a Bridger-type character — the guy knew everything. He made a great impact on the love of the outdoors. He made it interesting."

Davis said Sylvan's example led him to become a Scout leader. "There was a lot of respect," Davis said. "I learned from Scouting. I hope I can teach those kids what was taught to me."

In 1975, at age 68, Sylvan hiked at New Mexico's Philmont Scout Ranch with his Des Moines Scout Troop. (PHOTO FROM STEVE DAVIS)

As Sylvan's three younger sons reached high school age, they graduated to Explorer Post 201, which was one of the largest in the Central Iowa Council. Sylvan became an enthusiastic advisor to the outdoor-oriented youths.

"All our kids wanted to do was go backpacking," said Bill Darby, who headed the post committee. "So that's what Sy and I did." In addition to the Philmont trips, the Explorers hiked in Wyoming's Bridger Wilderness three times; in Isle Royale National Park, Lake Superior; in the Bob Marshall Wilderness, Montana; and in the Maroon Bells-Snowmass Wilderness, Colorado. The Scouts also made two canoe trips in the Quetico-Superior region of northern Minnesota and Ontario. Sylvan made his last Boy Scout canoe trip in 1983 at age 76, about six months after he'd had emergency heart bypass surgery.

When he was preparing for a trip, Sylvan regularly hiked around Des Moines to get into shape. "You could always see him, the years he was getting ready to go, in his training," Darby said. "He walked a 5-mile stretch… a regular route. You'd see him every morning out there."

Each Scout trip brought different memories. At the Maroon Bells-Snowmass Wilderness for example, it rained relentlessly for much of the week, Darby recalled. "The only dry spot in the whole damn wilderness was the piece of ground under the tents," he groaned.

To reach Isle Royale, the Scouts rode a ferry 25 miles in pea-soup fog. Once on the island, they battled clouds of mosquitoes, Darby said. But the plentiful moose, fearless foxes, and good fishing made the trip a wildlife bonanza. Darby still laughs about the moose that bellowed near their shelter, startling him and Sylvan from a sound sleep at 4 a.m. "You never saw Sy come out of a bunk so fast in all your life," he chuckled.

On the Scout outings, the only real concession made for Sylvan's leg was on the bus or train trip to the starting point, Darby said. Sylvan needed an aisle seat so his leg could stick out. Once on the trail, Sylvan declined any special treatment for his stiff leg, but the Scouts and Darby usually tried to have someone hike along with him when the rest of the crew went on ahead. Most boys considered it a privilege to hike with "Mr. Runkel."

"We always told them up front that Sy was gonna be [hiking] about a mile and a half an hour, and he was gonna be constant," Darby said. "I hiked with him a lot, and the kids hiked with him. He was so doggoned much fun to hike with because he was telling you stories. The kids just ate that up. He was teaching them, but they weren't aware they were being taught," Darby observed. "He was so smooth."

When the hikers sat down to rest, Sylvan usually remained standing. Only at the end of the day would he take the folding camp chair off his pack and sit down. "There was never any apology made or any expected," Darby said. "I think they respected him a great deal because he did what he did with that bum leg — and he did it as well as he did."

Sylvan's wilderness outings with Boy Scouts included several canoe trips to Minnesota's Boundary Waters Canoe Area.

The Scouts sometimes teased Sylvan for the world-class snoring that rumbled from his tent each night. He'd also poke fun at the boys.

"Did you see the rattlesnake?" he'd ask the unsuspecting hikers. When the youths looked startled, he feigned surprise. "Oh, you didn't see the rattlesnake? Well, the reason you didn't see it is because you went by it so fast!" Not sure whether to believe him or not, the energetic Scouts sometimes would slow down a little, Darby laughed. But the Scouts still rushed past an arrowhead that Sylvan picked up as he hiked methodically along a trail. Once again, he chided them good-naturedly for not noticing their surroundings.

Although teenage boys can try anyone's patience, Darby admired Sylvan's rapport with the Scouts. "I don't know that I ever heard Sy get mad at anybody," he marveled.

In 1985 the Mid-Iowa Council of the Boy Scouts gave Sylvan the Silver Beaver Award for his distinguished service to Scouting in the Des Moines area. The honor is the highest a Scouting council can bestow. But Sylvan was equally proud of the sterling silver belt buckle given to him by one group of Scouts after a memorable trip to Philmont.

Most of the Scouts eventually went their separate ways, but several

Wyoming's Bridger Wilderness lured Sylvan several times, including this 1976 trip with Explorer Scouts.

were reunited in January 1995 when they independently decided to attend Sylvan's memorial service. "I don't get real excited about funerals," said one, "but I felt I needed to show my respect to this man this way."

Although the boys may not have realized it at the time, they paid Sylvan an even greater tribute on a Philmont trip, as the troop was scaling Mount Baldy, the area's highest peak. As the eager teens scrambled to be first up the mountain, they suddenly realized who should lead the way. The Scouts held back, cheering for Sylvan, with his ranger's hat and walking stick, as he topped the summit.

CHAPTER 13

THE MOUNTAINEER

"IT'S NOT ABOUT CONQUERING; IT'S ABOUT ENJOYING OR JUST BEING AND APPRECIATING."

Playing on the Mississippi River bluffs near Moline, Sylvan got his first taste of climbing as a young boy. A few years later, on a family trip to Colorado, the teenager reveled in seeing real mountains and hiking a few tourist trails.

But not until 1925, on his hitchhiking trip with Mer Buhle, did Sylvan experience what it was like to scale a mountain on foot. Awestruck by Squaw Mountain, one of the first sights they encountered at the southeastern edge of Glacier National Park, the boys decided to climb the 7,280-foot peak. No matter that several other pinnacles in the park rise higher than 10,000

Sylvan's climbing exploits of the 1930s took him to the Grand Teton in Wyoming's rugged mountain ranges.

While preparing for a 1938 climb on Gannett Peak, the highest mountain in Wyoming, Sylvan laid out his gear to photograph for a possible magazine article.

feet: Sylvan and Mer were eager to tackle a mountain — any mountain.

As they headed up the slope, the novice climbers could barely put one foot ahead of the other. Their Illinois lungs couldn't get enough oxygen in the rarefied air of the Montana Rockies. Sylvan and Mer gave up their climb less than 500 feet from the summit. After two nights on the mountain, they headed for lower elevations to regain their strength. "We just weren't used to being in that thin air," Sylvan said.

But the mountains kept calling Sylvan. In 1927 he landed a job on the Windy Camp lookout tower in Oregon's Umpqua National Forest. The 20-year-old college student not only hiked up the 5,000-foot mountain with ease, but also packed all his water from a spring several hundred feet below. He regularly scampered up a 70-foot Douglas fir to a lookout platform atop the tree.

In the summers of 1931 and 1932 Sylvan again headed for the mountains of Montana and Idaho, where he worked fighting fires and on crews trying to eradicate white pine blister rust. He'd grown to love the high country.

By 1936 Sylvan yearned for bigger challenges. When Gilmour C. MacDonald, son of his Iowa State College forestry professor, invited him to climb the Grand Teton, Sylvan jumped at the chance. From a camp near the mountain the men took blankets and a little food, then hiked up a steep trail. When darkness fell, they slept on rocks near the base of the peak, preparing for the final climb. The next morning, they worked their way along a narrow ledge, but were stymied about 100 feet from the top by a sheer rock face.

Then the men spotted a long rope dangling enticingly in a natural chimney in the cliff. MacDonald pulled, and the rope held. Eagerly, they both pulled — then pulled again. The rope broke. Disheartened, the men headed down the mountain, frustrated by their failure but thankful they hadn't fallen.

The unsuccessful climb made Sylvan even more determined to reach his goal. On the descent he talked with other climbers and rangers who described a better route to the peak. Sylvan immediately began planning his next attempt to scale the mountain.

The following summer he and fellow SCS employee Floyd Harrison rode Harrison's Harley-Davidson motorcycle to Wyoming, drove the bike as far as they could into the foothills, then set off for the Grand Teton. On September 3, 1937, they succeeded in reaching the summit, even though the pleasant day turned to snow, hail, rain, and cold. But their victory cry was cut short by an ominous buzz.

"On arrival at top, we both got lightning shocks and electricity is humming all over the place!" Sylvan wrote in the logbook on the peak. This was no time to admire the scenery. With their hair standing up from static electricity, the men dropped to all fours and scrambled off the summit, lucky to avoid becoming lightning rods.

So what could be better than standing atop the Grand Teton? How about ascending Gannett Peak, the highest point in Wyoming? Sylvan and Harrison vowed to make the climb the next summer. They invited another SCS colleague, Joe Colgan, to join the party.

Sylvan ordered a new sleeping bag, a backpack, and other gear from L. L. Bean and Abercrombie and Fitch. To get into shape, he frequently asked Beulah to drive him out Iowa Highway 92 to Fontanelle, and he would walk the six miles home to Greenfield. Occasionally, he hiked the round-trip.

On an August Friday Sylvan headed west with Colgan and Harrison. After a full day at the office they left Greenfield at 9 p.m., drove straight through, and pulled into Jackson, Wyoming, at 11:30 the following night. Beulah, two female SCS employees, and Harrison's fiancée had driven ahead in another car and were waiting for the men. The next day, after touring Jackson and Grand Teton National Park, the women set out for a few days in Salt Lake City and Yellowstone National Park, while the men drove to a trailhead at Green River Lakes, near Pinedale.

Carrying 60-pound packs, Sylvan, Colgan, and Harrison hiked for two days to Summit Lake in the Wind River Range, where they caught a few fish and camped in the summer snow. After another day's hike and enduring a sleet storm, the men reached a trail crew's camp, where they happily accepted a supper of hot stew. As usual, they rolled their sleeping bags out under the stars. But Sylvan and his companions slept fitfully as fierce winds buffeted their campsite.

The next morning dawned clear and warmer, however, so the climbers gobbled a huge breakfast of sourdough pancakes, bacon, eggs, and coffee, then set out for Gannett Peak. Their spirits sagged only briefly when they encountered a glacier filling the valley between them and their destination. They roped themselves together and started across, listening apprehensively to the water running underneath and the occasional crack of shifting ice.

"It was pretty impressive if you've never climbed across a glacier," Sylvan admitted. "It filled the whole valley, about a mile across." After starting across the ice field, Colgan had second thoughts. He stopped on a rock outcrop to wait for his companions to return.

As Sylvan and Harrison approached the 13,804-foot summit, they followed a sharp ridge, keeping one foot on each side of the divide. They crept along for several hundred feet while looking down a sheer slope to a glacier that was between 2,000 and 3,000 feet below. The view from the top was even more spectacular.

"It really impresses you," Sylvan marveled years later. "Beautiful, beautiful country. Wild country. Not a sign of people or anything civilized at all up there. It's the wildest scene you can imagine," he declared.

"I never felt like I was in a wilderness anyplace else as much as I felt that I was in the middle of it there," Sylvan said. "All directions you look, it was just mountain peaks and glaciers as far as you could see. You're really alone. You get a different feeling. I would recommend it to anybody, if they want to really experience what wilderness is like."

Sylvan still hadn't gotten his fill of wild country. Studying maps of Wyoming, he keyed in on a rugged, roadless area about 60 miles wide between Pinedale and Dubois. That would be his next endeavor.

"So I decided I'd walk that by myself," he recounted later. "I thought it would be a good experience. When you're by yourself that way you see things that you won't see otherwise," he explained. "When you're walking along and you're talking to somebody, the wildlife can hear and the birds can hear, and they keep a low profile."

He loaded his cumbersome "Trapper Nelson" pack with 80 pounds of food and gear to prepare for his solo adventure. But Sylvan ended up discarding about half of the heavy supplies. He quickly discovered that hiking with such a massive pack wasn't much fun.

For two weeks Sylvan roamed the remote mountains and high country. Instead of true wilderness, however, he found rangeland with occasional cowboys tending their herds of cattle. He wondered whether his Colt Woodsman .22 pistol would protect him from a charging Hereford bull.

"And I found out what it's like to hike by yourself in the wilderness," he declared. "I would recommend it — some of the time. But a lot of the time it's kind of nice to have somebody else to visit with."

On one of his next climbing expeditions Sylvan took along some company. In 1939 he hiked up Middle Teton with Beulah's brother Silvian, or "Skiv," and Sylvan's 8-year-old son, Ramon. The trio climbed part way the first day, then camped on the mountain before reaching the peak on the second day. Ramon recalls wearing cowboy boots, sleeping in a cave,

sharing a sleeping bag with his father, eating canned pork and beans, and sliding down a long snowfield. Although Sylvan had to carry the youngster's pack partway, Ramon earned the distinction of being the youngest person to have reached the peak.

Having tasted the excitement of mountaineering, Ramon naturally was disappointed the next summer when his dad and a coworker, Vergil Webster, went back to the Tetons for more climbing. Neither Ramon nor Webster's son, Arnie, fully appreciated their alternative vacation — a trip to Chicago's Brookfield Zoo with their mothers.

Sylvan posed with a cutthroat trout he caught at Summit Lake, Wyoming, as proof that trout really can survive in alpine lakes.

When the United States entered World War II, Sylvan suddenly faced hurdles far bigger than mountaineering. After his D-Day glider crash, and during the three years of medical treatment on his broken left leg, he dared not even dream of being able to climb again.

When at last he learned that he could hike, hunt, and swim in spite of his injury, Sylvan once again began to look skyward. Mere mountains should not pose a major obstacle to a "survivor" like him. In 1969 with his sons Tom and Jon and other Boy Scouts, Sylvan hiked to the top of 12,441-foot Mount Baldy on the Philmont Scout Ranch in New Mexico. He later ascended Mount Baldy with Scout troops twice more, the last time in 1975 at age 68. In 1997 Tom's son, Ted, also climbed Mount Baldy with his father, to become the third generation of Runkels to have topped the peak.

Sylvan accompanied Scout troops on several other mountaineering adventures, including a hike to Summit Lake — the alpine lake where he'd camped in 1938 on his way to the top of Wyoming's Gannett Peak. Sylvan, Bernie, and several friends later backpacked in the mountains, including trips to the Wind River and Green River Lakes areas of Wyoming, and the Maroon Bells-Snowmass Wilderness in Colorado.

His father's example inspired Sylvan's son Tom. In 2001 Tom joined a

With Boy Scouts, family, and friends, Sylvan continued to hike mountainous areas of the West — such at Wyoming's Bridger Wilderness — despite his leg injury. (PHOTO BY BILL DARBY)

party of climbers that reached the top of the Grand Teton 64 years after Sylvan's ascent. Tom used a cell phone to make a surprise call to daughters Amy and Heather from the 13,770-foot summit.

Sylvan's spirit led others into the mountains, too. His granddaughter Rachael Hemstad climbed Mount Saint Helens as a young girl, then progressed to Mount Rainier and other U. S. peaks before moving to even more adventures in Mexico, Bolivia, Nepal, and Europe.

"But Denali was the big one," Rachael said. She led a successful all-woman climb of North America's highest point in 1995, the summer after Sylvan died. She had discussed her plans with "Pops," as she called Sylvan, and sensed her grandfather's concern for her safety. "He never said 'don't,'" Rachael recalled. "He just said, 'It's a real mean mountain.'"

Indeed, Denali unleashed "every kind of weather" during her party's 18-day climb, Rachael said. The five women fought wind, snow, and cold as they carried packs that weighed more than they did, slowly working their way up the mountain.

But Rachael felt as if Sylvan's spirit was guiding her. The climbers became "citizens" of the Denali community. They touched the earth, rock, ice, and soul of the mountain. "You have a spirit that is tied to the mountain... you have some kind of connection," Rachael said.

"And I definitely carry Sylvan on my shoulder," she said. "He's always sitting right there whispering little secrets in my ear."

On July 17 the weather improved, so the climbers started for the summit. "I was talking to the mountain, and I was talking to Grandpa; he was sittin' on my shoulder," Rachael said. "He was right there. And we got close to the summit and it just became glorious. We had weather like nobody's ever seen before. We had 70-plus degrees on the top of Denali. Unheard of!

"We had robin's egg–blue skies. We could see for miles. We spent over an hour on the summit. We had just an absolutely fabulous, fabulous, fabulous summit."

Rachael's mother, Marilyn Runkel Hemstad, credited Sylvan for Rachael's once-in-a-lifetime experience atop Denali. Marilyn vividly recalls Sylvan's words from his hospital bed, when the whole family realized he was dying:

"Now, you know, when I go, I don't know what's going to happen over there — but if there's anything that I can do for any of you, I'm going to do it!" Sylvan vowed.

"And he did!" Rachael exclaimed. Feeling her grandfather's presence, she stood at the top of the continent and shouted a salute they had shared: "To the sky! To the sky!"

During Sylvan's final years he loved to get Rachael's postcards telling of her most recent climbing experiences. Perhaps it was because Rachael articulated Sylvan's own feelings about the high, wild country. "And I've got his spirit, or at least I feel like I do," Rachael said. "There's something that is so absolutely wonderful about the mountains.

"You forget your worries, you forget everything, and just let your spirit go. There's something just magical. It's not about conquering; it's about enjoying or just being and appreciating."

CHAPTER 14

THE PILOT

"YOU'RE GONNA HAVE SOME TIMES WHEN YOU WONDER..."

Blame the Wright Brothers! Sylvan Runkel partly attributed his lifelong love of flying to a boyhood encounter with the fabled flying machine that Orville and Wilbur first coaxed into the air in 1903.

For a number of years after the first flight, the Wrights traveled the country to demonstrate their crude airplane. When they came to Jacksonville, Illinois, 5-year-old Sylvan joined a throng of eager spectators waiting for the air show in a pasture at the edge of town.

In 1940 Sylvan flew this Aeronca Chief 50 airplane in the "Ace of Clubs" flying club in Cedar Rapids, Iowa.

With great fanfare the Wrights revved up the engine. But the clumsy machine taxied down the runway, lifted a few feet into the air, then settled back down. The expectant crowd grew restless. Was this so-called flying machine a hoax? After a few more tries, however, the plane rose about 20 feet and traveled nearly 200 feet across the meadow.

"Everybody clapped and cheered," Sylvan recalled. "It was the beginning of the machine air age!" He paused, thinking of modern air travel. "It was a very humble beginning," he reflected.

A few years later, Sylvan's parents took him to the Illinois State Fair at Springfield for another flying demonstration. By then, planes had progressed to the point that they could fly a half mile or more. After circling the field, the pilot landed and was mobbed by excited onlookers. They started writing their names on the wings of the plane. Everybody sensed that history was being made — and they wanted to be a part of it.

Sylvan resolved that he, too, would fly. Even before he graduated from high school in 1924, he had earned enough money from his paper route and part-time jobs to take his first flying lessons. A chance glimpse of Charles Lindbergh in the *Spirit of St. Louis* in 1927 also fueled Sylvan's passion to fly.

During the summer of 1928, while working with his father in a factory in Moline, Sylvan saved enough money to take a few more lessons. He officially joined the air age when he soloed in Moline in a Lincoln Standard biplane. After watching Sylvan's bouncy landing, the instructor diplomatically suggested that his student could use a little more experience. Sylvan also had some flying instruction while he was in college at Ames. He recalled dryly that the World War I vintage "Jenny" was a nice plane — except for the minor fact that it would stall if the pilot attempted to climb and turn at the same time.

Although the $25 per hour cost of instruction kept him from earning his pilot's license for several years, Sylvan scraped together enough money even during the Depression to continue occasional flying lessons with M. L. Wearth in Ames. On summer Sunday afternoons he'd stop at the airport for a half-hour of flying.

Even if he couldn't find the time or money to fly, Sylvan often took Beulah, the kids, and their friends to the Des Moines airport to watch the planes. He pored over issues of *Popular Aviation*, fascinated with articles on gliders and on aerial photography. He persuaded his mother to take her first airplane ride in 1934. On at least one occasion Sylvan hitched a ride in *The Des Moines Register and Tribune's* plane, *Good News*, to inspect CCC projects in southern Iowa.

Sylvan earned his pilot's license in 1940, just two years after the creation of the Civil Aeronautics Authority. With flying still somewhat of a novelty, and grass (or dirt) runways common, many pilots paid little heed to legal restrictions that were beginning to regulate the use of aircraft.

The Runkel kids shared their father's fascination with flying. When Sylvan gave them rides, they would sit in the plane and shout "Contact!" as he stood on the ground and spun the propeller by hand to start the engine. "Ray and I were the only little kids in any of our classes who had ever flown in planes," Marilyn remembered. "But we had flown everywhere."

Sylvan and his SCS coworkers also realized the value of flying to get new perspectives on conservation problems and projects. Sylvan took hundreds of aerial photos for the agency or flew while other employees operated the camera.

Sylvan relished chances to give friends their first airplane rides. A few of those flights may have provided more excitement than either Sylvan or his passenger had bargained for. When Sylvan tried to take off to give SCS colleague Ray Currier his baptismal flight, the men discovered that the wings could not develop enough lift in the hot July air for the plane to get airborne. The aircraft bounced along a grassy pasture with no sign of leaving the ground.

"You know, Currier, I don't think we're gonna make it," Sylvan said, more or less calmly, before he brought the plane skidding to a halt at the end of the makeshift airfield.

"Even though we didn't get off the ground, it did provide quite a thrill," Currier recalled years later. "That tight new fence was awfully damned close when I climbed out!"

Coworker Oris Randolph was weeding his garden on a Saturday afternoon near Monticello, Iowa, when Sylvan buzzed him and shouted down from the plane, "Come out and get me!" Randolph met Sylvan in a pasture, and they took off again to photograph strip-cropping.

The flight became a joyride when Sylvan tried some stunts, such as climbing until the plane stalled, then diving again and leveling off. "I secretly hoped you knew what you were doing!" Randolph told Sylvan later. On another flight with Sylvan, the wind caught Randolph's glasses and blew them out the open window of the plane.

In the early 1940s Sylvan had another close call when he was piloting an Aeronca that belonged to the "Ace of Clubs" flying club in Cedar Rapids. While Sylvan was trying to land in a crosswind, the tail clipped a telephone pole beside the pasture. "WHAMBO!" Sylvan shouted, when describing the crash later. The plane pancaked into the ground from a height of about 20 feet.

"It shook me up a little bit," Sylvan conceded. He suffered a cut on his hand but no serious injuries. He and his fellow flying club members managed to repair the plane themselves. "It didn't cost me anything except my time — and my pride," he said sheepishly.

Sylvan's good fortune continued one fall evening when he and a coworker were flying a plane from Cedar Rapids to Monticello to prepare for the next day's aerial photography. Sylvan forgot to allow for shorter autumn days and found himself flying in darkness. He made several passes over the gravel roads near where he thought there was an open pasture.

Luckily, a farmer whose son was a pilot heard the low-flying plane and realized the problem. The quick-thinking man drove out in his

Sylvan often used his flying skills to take photos to illustrate conservation practices, such as contour farming near Greenfield. The SCS used many of those photos in their publications.

Model T to shine the car lights on a grassy landing area. "We came in right over him and held her straight," Sylvan said. "No problem at all — except we were all scared to death!"

Another aerial incident earned newspaper headlines for Sylvan and a new airport runway for Rockford, Illinois. Sylvan had offered to fly his supervisor's mother from Cedar Rapids to Rockford to make the trip easier for the woman, who was too frail to make the long journey by car. The flight went fine, but frantic airport workers waved off the plane as Sylvan attempted to land. Heavy rains had turned the landing strip into a quagmire. A pilot took off from a drier part of the field and led Sylvan to a nearby highway, where he dodged power lines and traffic to land safely on the paved road. As law officers arrived and began to "read me the riot act," Sylvan reminisced, local airport officials came to his defense. They explained that the plane could have crashed if he'd tried to land in the muddy field.

Local newspapers highlighted the story of how a grandmother had barely escaped a tragedy because of the inadequate airfield strip. The city promptly launched a fund-raising campaign to pave the runway.

On another flight over Illinois in the 1950s, when Sylvan and Bernie were returning from a glider pilots' reunion in Cleveland, Ohio, thickening clouds and rain forced his small plane lower and lower. Sylvan spotted a farmer's small, private airfield and was able to land as the weather deteriorated even further. After a night in a motel, the couple flew home to Ottumwa without mishap.

In retrospect, Sylvan shrugged off the incidents. "If you're gonna fly, you're gonna have some times when you wonder whether that was the best thing to do," he rationalized.

There was no wondering about his ill-fated D-Day flight, however. Next to the fact that Sylvan even survived that 1944 crash, it's almost as amazing that he continued to love small planes and flying for the rest of his life. He flew regularly until he was in his 70s.

Fate spared Sylvan in 1977 when a group of Iowans planned a trip to Alaska in several single engine airplanes. "They wanted me to go along, and I almost did," Sylvan said later. "But if I did, I wouldn't be here." Two of the eight planes crashed in a July 11 storm, killing Luther College professor and State Preserves Advisory Board member George Knudson and his wife, Shirley. Castalia farmer and conservationist Roy Schultz and his wife, Genevieve, along with four other people, also died.

Sons Ray and Tom inherited the flying bug and both earned pilot's licenses. Jeff also took a few flying lessons. Jeff recalls the regular Sunday afternoon ritual when Sylvan would rent a plane and take his sons flying. "Let's go upside down, Dad!" Jeff would beg. A few steep banks and rolls would appease the youngster without overly upsetting his mother on the ground.

Tom recalls the "impressive" experience of flying with Sylvan with the airplane doors open, then banking to look straight down at the ground 3,000 feet below. "I'd say he was a cautious pilot," Tom said, "but he liked to take things to the limit!"

Wade Hamor, an SCS employee who often flew with Sylvan, sometimes teased him about his meticulous safety checks. But Hamor openly welcomed the procedures. "His concentration was complete when piloting a plane," Hamor said. "I was always impressed with his attention to every detail."

Sylvan also maintained his sense of humor about flying. When one would-be passenger hesitated to take the flight, Sylvan reassured her: "Oh, don't worry! We'll get you down!" he declared.

CHAPTER 15

RETIREMENT

HE WAS DOING WHAT HE LOVED TO DO.

Sylvan Runkel retired from the SCS in 1972. He'd logged more than four decades of federal service, with jobs ranging from fighting forest fires, to hunting Japanese beetles, to flying military gliders, to planting trees, to mapping contour strips.

Some might have said he'd earned the right to relax a little, put his feet up, and watch the world go by. But Sylvan was not about to become a loafer. As he later joked in a letter to a friend who also was retiring, it's

Sylvan and Bernie, along with their black Labrador, Wiezie, often visited their cabin on the shore of Lake Superior near Grand Marais, Minnesota.
(PHOTO BY KARISA RUNKEL)

hard to give up a job that you've been devoted to for much of your life.

"Your many years of dedication to your work will give you a little trouble when you try to do something else," Sylvan wrote, "but persist — and maybe you can overcome the old habits. I haven't been able to do it yet," he confided, "but next year I'll try again!"

He didn't try very hard. Instead, for two decades after his retirement, he continued to give hundreds of programs and lead countless nature hikes for garden clubs, civic groups, and conservation organizations. "He didn't say 'no' very often" when asked to speak, said Bernie, recalling her husband's full appointment calendar. Sylvan also received a steady stream of requests to inventory plants or prepare environmental reports for public and private groups.

Bernie also kept busy. With college expenses looming for their three sons, she went back to work part-time teaching General Educational Development (GED) classes in a number of Des Moines–area schools. She still found time to accompany Sylvan on many of his trips.

One of Sylvan's most rewarding experiences came in the late 1970s, when Iowa Public Television invited him to participate in their "Iowa Wildlife" and "Land Between Two Rivers" series. He devoted many long days to several IPTV productions over the span of about 10 years. His face, hat, voice, and walking stick grew more familiar to many Iowans.

State Ecologist Dean M. Roosa worked with Sylvan on the State Preserves Advisory Board and later coauthored *Wildflowers of the Tallgrass Prairie* and *Wildflowers and Other Plants of Iowa Wetlands.*

Perhaps Sylvan's best-known projects were the wildflower guides he co-authored. First came *Wildflowers of Iowa Woodlands*, with Al Bull in 1979. The two men also wrote similar guides for Illinois and Indiana. In 1989 Sylvan and state ecologist Dean Roosa completed *Wildflowers of the Tallgrass Prairie*. The naturalist friends then began work on *Wildflowers and Other Plants of Iowa Wetlands*. Sylvan died before the two men could finish, but Roosa saw the project to completion in 1999.

Each of the books

revealed Sylvan's fascination with people's uses of plants. For nearly every species, he tried to give examples of how Native Americans and pioneers depended on plants for food, medicine, fiber, or dye. He gleaned much of the information from an old series of Milwaukee Public Museum bulletins based on the accounts of Native American medicine men.

Their unique approach made the wildflower guides quite popular, said IPTV producer Tom Moore. "A lot of the books identify the flower or the plant," he said, "but in Sylvan's books, it talks about them in a human way." Sylvan explained how plants meet certain human needs, Moore said. "It makes a human connection, and then the next step is how does it relate to the human condition," Moore said. "It's relationships . . . to the world and what that means."

When asked about the significance of the prairie book, Sylvan told a story of a pioneer girl whose teacher asked her to define heaven. The youngster quickly responded: "Heaven would be when I asked somebody what a flower is and they could tell me!"

Sylvan and Roosa drew on their combined natural history and communication skills in preparing the field guides. The men often worked together, stacking their references on the Runkel dining room table. "His office was too crowded to work in," Roosa joked. "[It was] filled with awards and other mementos of a lifetime of association with nature and naturalists."

Sylvan and Roosa began to work on the prairie book in the early 1980s, while Roosa was ecologist for the State Preserves Advisory Board and Sylvan was a member of the board. The men spent many hours traveling the state, talking to landowners, and exploring natural areas. Sylvan "was a joy to be in the field with," Roosa said.

"He and [the late] Larry Eilers [a University of Northern Iowa botanist who also was a good friend of Sylvan] were two people who got more enjoyment out of botanizing," Roosa declared. "A lot of people, if it isn't a new plant or a rare plant, or if it's a weed, they don't really think it's very neat. But they could take the most common plant and tell you a story about it. They just truly enjoyed plants."

Roosa admired Sylvan's intelligence and his diverse interests, which included mythology and the classics, poetry, and Iowa State University football. Roosa chuckled about Sylvan's fascination with the *Star Wars* movie, and how Sylvan went to great length to describe the film's robot hero, R2D2.

Sylvan found a special delight in food — especially pie and cinnamon rolls. Sylvan was truly chagrinned when he tried to take Roosa to a cafe that served ground cherry pie, only to find that the place had closed. When telling stories, Sylvan seldom failed to comment on the food. He spoke of the oatmeal he ate on his 1925 hitchhiking trip, the K rations he carried on D-Day, the doughnuts served to wounded soldiers in military hospitals, and the dehydrated meals on Boy Scout trips.

Although Sylvan earned modest royalties from the wildflower guides, he gave away dozens of copies. Profits weren't nearly as high a priority as getting people acquainted with the outdoors. An avid reader himself, Sylvan often shared other books, essays, and new ideas with friends and acquaintances, Roosa said.

That passion for knowledge made Sylvan an inspiration to friends and colleagues, such as other members of the Preserves Board, said Dorothy Baringer, who served on the board with him. "His schedule of talks, field trips, and Boy Scout programs filled his calendar. He was always happy to share his knowledge and time," Baringer said. "I became convinced that the way to be happy and content after retirement is to contribute of one's time and talent in the community and state in which we live."

Sylvan also was determined to be self-sufficient. On a Preserves Board field trip, Baringer offered her hand as Sylvan was trying to climb a steep slope — but he politely declined her help. "Dorothy, if I don't do it, I can't do it," Sylvan said resolutely.

His retirement and advancing age didn't dampen the contagious, youthful enthusiasm that had characterized Sylvan throughout his life. In 1974, while surveying plants at the site of a proposed drainage project near Gowrie, Iowa, Sylvan happened upon a grooved stone ax left by Native Americans along an ancient lakeshore. He shouted with excitement for his companions to come see what he'd found.

"He was dancing up and down. He was beside himself," laughed Howard Jensen of Fort Dodge, who still smiles at the image of Sylvan on the hillside, wearing his ranger hat and hopping with jubilation.

Sylvan also could get enthusiastic about more ordinary discoveries. Jensen's wife, Barbara, recalled Sylvan's visit to their secluded home. His first words were: "Joe Pye weed!"

"Who else could get that excited over Joe Pye weed?" Barbara Jensen marveled. Sylvan also charmed the Jensens with tales of the jewelweed and bedstraw he found in their yard. "His cost for supper was he had to tell us what our weeds were," Barbara said. (Sylvan hardly ever called them "weeds," however; they were merely plants out of place.)

But if retirement meant traveling Iowa to help people identify those plants, Sylvan thrived on it, observed his good friend Bob Moorman of Ames. "He was as busy as ever or busier," Moorman said. "He did it all."

The two men had worked together on conservation and education projects for more than 20 years while Moorman was extension wildlife specialist for Iowa State University and Sylvan was an SCS biologist. But "Sy didn't have to ask too many questions" about the natural world, Moorman said.

These two naturalists continually honed their skills. When traveling to workshops or field days, they'd have contests to see who could identify the most trees through the windshield of a speeding car. White oak or bur oak? Bitternut hickory or American elm? Fir or pine? Aspen or cottonwood?

Sylvan had sought Moorman's help when they first met in the 1950s. At that time, Sylvan had a better grasp of the prairie flora, while Moorman specialized in woodland flowers. The two tutored each other on wildflower identification. Later, when Sylvan and Bull were writing the woodland wildflower guides, Moorman suggested listing the flowers in the order that they bloomed. That became the format for the prairie and wetlands guide, as well.

Although Sylvan wrote numerous magazine articles and information sheets for the SCS, as well as the later wildflower guides, he preferred the spoken word, Moorman observed. "He was more interested in educating them face to face."

Thus, Sylvan built his reputation on field trips and lectures. Even the popular wildflower books were no substitute for a real-life nature hike with Sylvan. And he never seemed to tire of the outings. "He was doing what he loved to do," Moorman said. "And I think that showed to his audiences."

On most of his field trips Sylvan carried a walking stick and donned his ranger's hat. He often wore a plaid shirt and sometimes

In his later years, Sylvan sported a full, white beard. He liked to wear reds and plaids. (PHOTO BY LARRY A. STONE)

added a string tie. His Sierra cup hung from his belt, and his Nikkormat camera in its black leather case was slung over his shoulder. He frequently stopped to take pictures, especially when visiting a new area.

Delores Larson of Fort Dodge met Sylvan on a group nature hike that turned out to be "the most fascinating day I ever spent. You could ask him anything and he knew the answer," she said. She realized that all her companions also were engrossed in Sylvan's presentation. "I'd never seen a group of people be so quiet," Larson said.

"Sylvan Runkel was always the eager communicator," said former State Forester Gene Hertel, who became both a personal and professional friend. Hertel told of a trip to Europe that he and his late wife, Elsie, took with Sylvan and Bernie in 1979. They visited the beaches of Normandy, near where Sylvan had landed on D-Day.

"Sy got into a conversation with a local Frenchman," Hertel said. "In spite of the language barrier, the conversation went on for about an hour. The Frenchman was gesturing toward various spots along the coast and talking rapidly in the gathering dusk. Sy probably understood more of what was being communicated than one would think," Hertel said. "He had an intense desire to grasp the other's meaning and to relate it to his own experience. But who, other than Sy, would have had the patience to continue such a conversation? Part of it was his wanting to know what was being said. Perhaps more, it was his desire to let the other man know they shared an emotional tie to that place and another time," Hertel suggested.

After that European trip, which also included visits to Germany's Black Forest and Runkel Castle, Sylvan enrolled in a German class at Drake University. He studied the language with other students young enough to be his grandchildren.

When Sylvan was nominated to be president of the Iowa Academy of Science in 1977, his good friend Karl E. "Gene" Goellner, a retired Coe College biology professor, was embarrassed to be the opposing candidate. The two white-whiskered biologists joked about awarding the title to the one with the scraggliest beard. Goellner won the office, and Sylvan wholeheartedly congratulated him on the congenial race.

Goellner, likewise, respected Sylvan's woods wisdom, calling him "one of the friendliest and most capable naturalists I ever knew. He was full of insightful comments about some detail to be noticed, or about some broader concept that we shouldn't overlook."

On a visit to the Goellners' home near Hayward, Wisconsin, Sylvan praised a patch of unusual woodland wildflowers, declaring it "as fine a stand of wild sarsaparilla as I've ever seen." From one biologist to another, that's a compliment!

Sylvan never — well almost never — expressed anger. Former Iowa State University botany professor Roger Q. "Jake" Landers witnessed one rare display of ire when Sylvan and other Iowa Academy of Science members toured the academy's farm near Reinbeck. To their dismay, they found that the tenant had secretly kept hogs in the woodlot. Most of the trees were damaged and many were killed.

"I never saw Sy as mad as he was during the visit when the damage was discovered," Landers said. "The idea of hogs among the trees was something he never expected a sane person to do."

One of Sylvan's few other displays of wrath came at Philmont Scout Ranch when a rock-climbing instructor carelessly allowed a Scout to fall. Sylvan first tended to the boy's injuries, which luckily were not serious, then told the guide in unmistakable language that there was no excuse for such a safety lapse. Sylvan's son Tom, who witnessed the incident, said his father was appalled to think that the instructor had endangered the young boys he was supposed to be teaching.

Roosa often told of an incident when he and Sylvan visited a natural area only to discover that the landowner had bulldozed and destroyed the unique site. While Roosa could not contain his rage, Sylvan quietly shook his head in dismay at the farmer's ignorance. "Dag nab! I think he's on the wrong track!" Sylvan lamented.

Bernie shared Sylvan's love of travel and the mountains, including Old Squaretop, a peak that overlooks Green River Lakes, north of Pinedale, Wyoming.

"That was typical of Sy," Roosa said. "He was either genetically or philosophically incapable of thinking bad thoughts about people."

Sylvan remained active and vigorous after his retirement, refusing to let his old war injury get him down. He and Bernie backpacked with several friends in Wyoming's Bridger Wilderness and in the Maroon Bells-Snowmass Wilderness in Colorado in the 1970s. He also had accompanied Boy Scout troops on several wilderness trips.

When Sylvan suffered chest pains after deer hunting in December 1982, he was reluctant to admit that he might need to visit a hospital for the first time since he was discharged from the military in 1947. He suffered a heart attack while cardiologists were examining him, and surgeons performed emergency bypass surgery.

Although he was 76 years old, Sylvan recovered from the heart procedure quickly enough to accompany a Boy Scout troop on a wilderness trip in the Boundary Waters Canoe Area the next summer. He made several more trips to the Boundary Waters in following years.

"Did you bring the peaches?" became Sylvan's standard greeting to his friends Don and Kay Wall of Ames, after one of those canoe trips. The Walls had packed the food — including peaches in tin cans, which are banned in the wilderness area. When rangers stopped the party to check for illegal containers, Sylvan charmed the young officers with tales of the North Woods, and talked them out of issuing a citation.

His wilderness travels were curtailed a few years later when Sylvan developed a leg inflammation that doctors blamed on a flare-up of the bone infection he'd contracted from the D-Day injuries. This time, physicians successfully treated the ailment by inserting a catheter into his chest to inject regular doses of antibiotics from a pouch Sylvan carried.

In 1989, at age 82, Sylvan had another close call with heart problems. He was rushed to the hospital after collapsing at an SCS retirees breakfast. The doctor told Sylvan he was dying. Sylvan accepted the prognosis and urged his family not to worry. He began telling a story about how Native Americans sometimes placed their dead chiefs on tree branches for a funeral ceremony.

Family members could not face the prospect of losing their patriarch, however. They changed doctors and treatments and Sylvan rebounded. He lived another five years. During that time he was strong enough to fly to Seattle, Washington, to visit his daughter Marilyn, to travel to a glider pilots reunion in Texas, and to make several trips to his Lake Superior cabin at Grand Marais, Minnesota.

Even when he had to forgo strenuous outdoor activities, Sylvan continued to play the piano, as he had since boyhood. Companions often persuaded him to play old favorites, pop songs, or even classical tunes on any available keyboard. When Sylvan found a piano and started playing, people listened.

The late Jack Borg recalled a 1984 stop at an Alaska youth hostel with Sy and Bernie and several other friends. "Sylvan got down at the piano and started playing his ragtime tunes... and gradually accumulated quite a crowd," Borg said. A tourist from Denmark joined in with an accordion, and the party got even livelier. "Everybody was supposed to be in bed by 10 o'clock," Borg laughed. "But not that night!"

Sylvan loved to sit on the porch of his cabin, where he could savor the sights, sounds, and smells of the North Shore natural community.

People from all walks of life recognized Sylvan Runkel. Once, while he and Bernie were driving on Interstate Highway 80, an Iowa State Trooper made a U-turn and flashed his red lights to signal them to stop. When the grinning patrolman approached the car, he asked Sylvan when the men could go deer hunting together again.

Beth Brown of Osceola, who'd been on nature hikes with Sylvan and had seen his wildflower programs, books, and TV specials, once encountered Sy and Bernie in a shopping mall. Brown rushed over to the Bernie and blurted, "I'm in love with your husband!"

"I am, too!" Bernie retorted with a laugh.

Sylvan showed an honest interest in other people, said Moore, the TV producer. "Every time that I talked to him, he somehow remembered my wife's name and my son's name and what was going on."

Larry Benne of Sioux City was touched by the compassion Sylvan displayed when Benne's wife, Carolyn, died in 1980. Sylvan and the Bennes shared an enthusiasm for environmental education and they had become close friends. When Carolyn died suddenly, Larry took particular solace from Sylvan, who could relate to the feelings of having lost a spouse. "He was a caring, respectful listener," Larry Benne said.

Sylvan took great pleasure in his 16 grandchildren and eight great-grandchildren and never tired of repeating his stories of hitchhiking, fighting fires, mountain climbing, or other adventures for his family to hear.

"His stories made a little happening into a wonderful event," said Karisa Runkel, daughter of Sylvan's oldest son, Ramon. "And each time it was as if you were hearing it for the first time."

CHAPTER 16

A CABIN
ON A LAKE

"YOU OUGHT TO GO UP TO THE NORTH SHORE AND STAY AT MY CABIN."

As much as Sylvan Runkel loved Iowa and Illinois, his boyhood haunts along the Mississippi River, and the mountainous expanses of the West, he often found himself drawn northward, to what he sometimes described as "the most beautiful place I can think of."

Tucked back from the shore of Lake Superior about 12 miles north of Grand Marais, Minnesota, off a sandy trail jokingly named "Sylvan Strasse," sits a plywood cabin. The sign over

To Sylvan, the Lake Superior beach in front of his cabin north of Grand Marais, Minnesota, was "the most beautiful place I can think of."

the door proclaims "Runkel Schloss," but the German word for castle may be a bit of a stretch. "It's a shack, mostly," Sylvan admitted.

Unlike many other second homes scattered along the North Shore, this cabin is all but invisible from the lake — which, of course, means there is no panoramic view of the water. But Sylvan planned it that way. He shuddered at the thought of intruding on the wildness of the big lake, or

Nearly hidden by vegetation, Sylvan's "trapper's cabin" sits along the shore of Lake Superior, northeast of Grand Marais, Minnesota. (Photo by Ben Graham)

on the scenery of the North Shore. His son Jeff recalled Sylvan's dismay when a ruffed grouse scolded work crews who were beginning to build the cabin. The people had invaded the bird's habitat.

To experience the lake, visitors to the cabin first must listen to the whistling of the wind in the birches and smell the balsam firs. Invariably, the sound of pounding waves will lure them down to the shore. Only a faint trail leads over the bedrock — a billion-year-old lava flow where sphagnum, lichens, blueberries, and twinflowers now cling to pockets of soil.

At the edge of the lake, crystal waters wash the brown gravel beach where occasional rock hounds stroll in search of agates. The breakers have scoured the shore, tossing smooth pebbles into undulating drifts between low outcrops of dark, volcanic basalt. A few tufts of beach grass cling to cracks in the rock. But just beyond the reach of the crashing surf, lavender beach pea blossoms dot the edge between the shore and the woodlands, tickling the roots of a line of alders.

Between the lake and the vegetation lies an assortment of driftwood, tossed up by frequent storms. Like the rocks, the chunks of wood have been polished smooth by the relentless water. Shreds of birch bark and sticks of beaver-chewed aspen await only a lighted match to fuel a campfire. On a cool summer evening, as the flames dance and darkness engulfs the lake, it's easy to imagine a bearded figure in a ranger's hat

SYLVAN T. RUNKEL

smiling out from the shadows as youngsters toast marshmallows over the coals.

As the fire dies, the stars grow brighter overhead, with no competition from streetlights, security lights, or headlights. A Great Bear — the Big Dipper — crouches on the treetops above the shore, while the Little Bear peers shyly from the blackness. Someone picks out the sprawling "W" of Cassiopeia, and the stargazers marvel at the uncountable pinpoints of light from the Milky Way. The hypnotic lapping of water on rocks, the magic of the glowing coals, and the dark, celestial splendor cast a spell on the human intruders.

The big lake also communicates nature's awesome power. Sylvan and Bernie often talked of visiting the North Shore in November, as winter approached. When his son Ramon questioned the timing, Sylvan tried to imagine the cold winds buffeting the lake.

"Yes!" said Sylvan. "I want to go up there when it's really storming. I want to watch the waves come crashing in and hit the shore!"

No matter what the season, Sylvan loved his two-acre hideaway — and he loved to share it with others. "You ought to go up to the North Shore and stay at my cabin" was the standard invitation to dozens of friends and acquaintances. Many accepted the hospitality.

When Jean C. Prior, senior research geologist with the Iowa Department of Natural Resources, visited the cabin, she was captivated by the unobtrusive structure that blended so well into the surroundings. "It just looks like him," Prior said.

Howard and Barbara Jensen of Fort Dodge, who got to know Sylvan through their work with The Nature Conservancy, joked about the deer mice that shared their quarters during their visits. "You'd hear them gnawing all night long," Barbara laughed.

Steve Lekwa, director of the Story County Conservation Board, chanced to meet Sylvan and Bernie in a Grand Marais restaurant late in the summer of 1993. Sylvan was headed home, but he insisted on delaying his trip to take Lekwa to his little bit of lakeshore.

Sylvan proudly showed him where moose crossed on the nearby highway, then led him to the secluded cabin. "You almost bumped into the wall before you knew it was there," said Lekwa. "It looked like it had been helicoptered in."

What began as a brief tour became a full-fledged nature hike, despite Bernie's concern that her 87-year-old husband might not have the stamina

Sylvan's wooden fishing boat, Maud, near his cabin on Trout Lake, Minnesota, about 1960.

to explore the rugged rocks and woodlands. "He started sneaking for the Superior lakeshore, and before we were done, we were down there!" Lekwa said.

Sylvan delighted in pointing out the bunch-berries, mountain ash, Clintonia, asters, club mosses, gold thread, Indian pipe, yellow birches, fireweed, salmon berries, and the rich variety of other North Woods plants along the lake. He and Lekwa nibbled raspberries as they basked in the solitude. Sylvan hated to leave without introducing Lekwa to just one more "citizen."

Tom Moore, a producer at Iowa Public Television, had known Sylvan only a couple of months when Moore happened to mention that he and his wife planned to vacation on the North Shore of Lake Superior.

"I've got a cabin there," Sylvan said excitedly. Then he proceeded to draw a map to the site, and almost insisted that Moore stay there. He took special care to explain how to find the rustic outhouse. "Don't let the bear scratches on the door bother you!" Sylvan told Moore, as he described the crude biffy. "He was serious!" Moore laughed. "There were big claw marks on the door."

When Moore arrived at the property and began to explore the Lake Superior shoreline, neighbors came out to check on the visitors. "They said, 'Oh you're a friend of Sylvan's' — and that's all there was to it," Moore said. "They all knew him, and they figured if I was a friend of Sylvan's I was going to be all right!"

Although Sylvan adored the primitive setting of his lakeshore "shack," he enjoyed occasional luxuries, as well. Ben Graham, professor emeritus of biology at Grinnell College, was visiting the Runkels at the rustic cabin when Bernie suggested it was time for "high tea." Graham and the Runkels promptly drove a few miles up Highway 61 for afternoon tea and sweets at The Naniboujou Lodge. The exclusive resort, built in the 1920s as a private club for celebrities (Babe Ruth, Jack Dempsey and Ring Lardner were charter members), is as elegant as Sylvan's cabin is modest and unassuming. Decorated in Cree Indian motif, the lodge was named for a friendly spirit who Native American folklore said had chased the devil from the North Shore.

For all its quiet seclusion and beauty, however, Sylvan built the North Shore cabin because he and his family were forced to move from Trout Lake, north of Lake Vermilion, Minnesota. Sylvan had discovered Trout Lake while he was on medical leave from a military hospital in 1945, when he and his first wife, Beulah, stayed with friends from Ames who had a lot there. (They were on their way home on V-J Day, August 14, 1945, when the sirens in a northern Minnesota town celebrated Japan's surrender and the end of the war.)

Several subsequent trips to Trout Lake helped Sylvan to cope with his war injuries and readjust to civilian life. The borrowed cabin wasn't fancy — Sylvan got so frustrated with the hordes of mice that he shot at them with his .22 pistol — but he grew so fond of the spot that he and Beulah bought two lots on the lake in 1947. Although Beulah died two years later, Sylvan's dream of his own cabin on Trout Lake eventually came true.

In 1954 Sylvan hired Orie LaPointe, a carpenter from Ottumwa, to help him build the cabin. Bernie and Karen joined in the project, while baby Tom stayed with Bernie's mother in Iowa. Bernie's cousin Bill Eden and a high school friend helped with the heavy lifting. In subsequent years the family continued to add refinements to the vacation retreat. The comfortable,

Ramon, Bernie, Orie LaPointe, Karen, and family dog, George, at their Trout Lake cabin about 1954.

Sylvan at his cabin on Trout Lake, Minnesota, in 1962.

one-room building eventually included spacious cupboards, a wood-burning kitchen stove, a propane refrigerator, a ladder to a sleeping loft — "and the nicest outhouse on Trout Lake," Bernie laughed.

Just getting there was an adventure. First came the drive to Arrowhead Point on Lake Vermilion, followed by a ride to the Trout Lake portage in "Maud," a 14-foot wooden boat with a 7.5-horsepower Martin outboard. A flatbed truck, which backed into the water to load boats, hauled the gear across the portage to Trout Lake. After another six-mile boat ride, past a series of islands the family called "The Five Sisters," travelers could pull up to Norway Point. The cabin sat behind a little island that sheltered it from winds that swept across Trout Lake.

Ramon and his wife, Carla, built a dock while spending their honeymoon there in 1956. Many other family members tell stories of fishing, swimming, and berry-picking at the cabin, where they would vacation in late August each year. The lake retreat offered an escape from Iowa's heat and hay fever season, along with a wild spot for the family to relax.

Deer often stole along a trail near the cabin, and other wildlife shared the woods. When Jeff was about 5, he woke up in the middle of the night and matter-of-factly announced that a bear and two cubs were blocking his route to the outhouse.

A big patch of blueberries on the point nearly always ripened about the time the family came to Trout Lake for Sylvan's August 30 birthday, prompting the tradition of birthday blueberry pie. Sylvan also loved to make pancakes for breakfast. Bernie recalled how he would sprinkle the batter with blueberries and add extra sugar and eggs so the flapjacks would brown better. He entertained the kids by flipping the pancakes into the air to turn them.

Sons Tom, Jon, and Jeff couldn't wait for the summer trips to Trout Lake, where they roamed the woods or caught rock bass off the dock. Often, they'd go fishing with their dad, and the whole family would spend the day on the lake. Sylvan frequently fried fresh fish for lunch, while Bernie baked biscuits in a reflector oven. "I usually took a can of Spam in case nobody caught fish," Bernie joked.

In the evening, when people were relaxing around the campfire, mysterious shrieks, howls, and growls sometimes floated out of the blackness beyond the firelight. When someone turned to ask Sylvan what the noises might be, he never could be found. By the time he reappeared, eyes twinkling mischievously, the woods would be quiet again.

Sylvan loved "the wonder of discovery," said his daughter Prasannata. When he found a lady's slipper orchid at Trout Lake, he came into the cabin whispering about the treasure he wanted to share. "We went out in the woods and came up to it softly and quietly and were so surprised by it. Not just, 'Tromp, tromp, here it is,' but the whole approach: 'Ahhh, look at this lady's slipper.' It was like the child in him."

The Runkels and their guests loved the solitude of the cottage on the lake. But wilderness advocates such as Sigurd Olson, Aldo Leopold, and other conservation leaders whom Sylvan admired also recognized the unique qualities of Trout Lake and northern Minnesota's lake country. In 1965, after a heated debate, Congress forced private owners to sell their land to create the Boundary Waters Canoe Area. While he supported long-term protection of the region from future development, Sylvan still lamented the loss of his own little patch of backcountry.

Reluctantly, Sylvan and his family removed most of their furniture and personal belongings, but a massive old cookstove was too much to handle. When the family originally acquired the kitchen range, Ramon had hauled it to the boat landing in the back seat of his 1946 Mercury convertible. But nobody could face the prospect of lugging the heavy wood-burner back to civilization. The stove stayed in the cabin even when federal workers finally took the structure out onto the ice to burn. The stove, some nails, and a few ashes sank to the lake bottom the following spring.

Although the Runkels have grown very fond of their new retreat on Lake Superior, some family members regularly return to Trout Lake,

Sons Tom (left) and Jon share Sylvan's excitement over two lake trout they caught in Trout Lake.

where they canoe or boat out to Norway Point for a picnic and reminiscing. White pines and other vigorous young trees now grow where the cabin once stood, but a rusted bolt imbedded in a rock marks the site of the dock. Lake trout still lurk in the deep hole off Trout Rock. Kids still can pick blueberries along the point, and bears prowl the woods. And Sylvan's spirit just may be watching, to be sure the kids and bears don't end up in the same berry patch.

CHAPTER 17

CONSERVATION LEADER

"HE HELD US RESPONSIBLE WITHOUT EVER LECTURING US."

From the "Knights of the Square Table," which Sylvan organized with boyhood friends, to presidency of the Iowa State College Forestry Club, to high offices in state and national conservation groups, Sylvan's peers looked to him for leadership.

He served as president of the Iowa chapters of the Soil Conservation Society of America, the Society of American Foresters, and The Wildlife Society. Sylvan was the only person to have headed all three groups. He also helped to organize the Iowa Conservation Education Council, the Iowa Association of Naturalists, and the Iowa Natural History Association. As a board member of the Iowa Chapter of The Nature Conservancy, Sylvan's tireless work for natural areas earned him the national organization's highest honor, the Oak Leaf Award.

Hikers explore the Sylvan Runkel State Preserve in the Loess Hills of Monona County, Iowa.
(PHOTO BY LARRY A. STONE)

Ida Ruth Miller (rear) and Joyce Farquharson helped Sylvan plant a sycamore tree at Living History Farms.

Yet Sylvan may have led most effectively in less formal roles, when he was simply helping others to "get acquainted" with the wonders of nature. "If we get acquainted with natural communities, we feel at home," he said. "Anyplace we feel at home, we feel like protecting."

Sylvan's low-key but solid guidance played a major part in building interest in western Iowa's Loess Hills. "This is the kind of country I like — something that hasn't been spoiled too much," Sylvan said of the hills. Thanks to Sylvan and others, the region gained prominence throughout the last quarter of the 20th century.

Much of the momentum grew from the Loess Hills Prairie Seminar, held annually near Onawa, Iowa. Although Sylvan missed the first seminar in 1977, he attended nearly every successive event until the early 1990s, when his health no longer would permit the strenuous hikes.

The Loess Hills had intrigued Sylvan long before many of the current seminar-goers were born. A photo taken about 1940 shows Sylvan on an overlook, gazing out across the hills. He also studied Loess Hills plant communities and tested soil to show that prairies originally grew where trees now cover some hills.

At the seminar, Sylvan's nature hikes regularly drew the largest crowds. "It was kind of like a magnetic attraction," said Ed Brogie, a Laurel, Nebraska, science teacher who annually brought students to the workshop. So many people wanted to be with Sylvan that other speakers often had very small audiences. "It was like prime-time TV. Nobody wanted to be opposite him!" joked one naturalist. Sylvan was embarrassed by his own popularity.

But Sylvan, the teacher, also enjoyed being a student. "He was always willing to learn something new," said Brogie, an ornithologist who fielded Sylvan's many questions about birds. "You could tell he really cared," Brogie added. It "was not just a job, it was a passion."

Seminar participants still speak of Sylvan in hallowed tones. A bench on a ridge overlooking the seminar site is inscribed "Sylvan Runkel."

Hikers who stop to rest on the wooden bench sometimes feel they are sharing the seat with a quiet man in a ranger's hat who's eager to tell a story about another Loess Hills "citizen."

At the Dorothy Pecaut Nature Center in the Loess Hills of Stone State Park in Sioux City, one room is dedicated to Sy and Bernie Runkel. Fittingly, the space is used by Woodbury County Conservation Board volunteers and interns who teach and do service work at the center. The space was made possible by a donation from William and Dianne Blankenship of Sioux City, who worked with Sylvan on the Loess Hills Prairie Seminar.

The highest tribute to Sylvan's connections to the Loess Hills came in 1996 when a 330-acre tract adjacent to the seminar grounds was dedicated as the Sylvan Runkel State Preserve. A few years before, Sylvan had explained to people at the seminar why the region is so special.

"When you come into the Loess Hills, you get the feeling that you are immersing yourself into an ancient, yet vibrantly alive and on-going historical panorama of wild nature," Sylvan said. "You not only feel it! You see it! All around you! What power those hurricane force winds had — to pile up these tremendous hills of wind-blown soil…. And what a tremendous and powerful army of green plants moved in to colonize, cover and protect those great hills of the wind." People followed — from Native Americans, to Lewis and Clark, to pioneers, Sylvan said.

"And now us! And we can still find the same kinds of plants that Lewis and Clark found and used. These are not dead museum specimens! These are living natural citizens — who are carrying on the traditional work of the prairie community. Here we have a natural, living history book," Sylvan said.

Another of Sylvan's favorite projects was the restoration of an overgrazed woodland and small stream along the Miller Nature Trail at Living History Farms near Des Moines. Ida Ruth Miller of Des Moines led the effort in memory of her husband, Wayne Miller, with the goal of re-creating a landscape like the pioneers had found.

"I think Sylvan saw this as a tremendous opportunity to coax it back to its natural state," said Steve Green, former director of Living History Farms. "He was watching and teaching us to watch. It was like we all were going to watch it turn back into a woods."

Beginning in 1981 Sylvan worked with Ida Ruth Miller and other volunteers to build footbridges across the stream and plant wildflowers in the woodlands. He never missed the annual workday. The Runkel and

Miller families and their friends have continued the project, with more planting each year.

Sylvan also advised the Iowa Natural Heritage Foundation and Iowa Humanities Board in a project to design the Native American (Ioway) village at Living History Farms. Because Sylvan had studied native plants and their food and medicinal uses by Native Americans, "he was a living link," Green said. "He was just such a tremendous resource," not only with information but also with encouragement, Green said. "It simply would not have come about without him being involved."

From 1969 to 1979 Sylvan took on a more formal role as a member of the State Preserves Advisory Board, including two years as its chair. Dorothy Baringer of Woodburn served with him on the board, which is charged with protecting the state's most precious natural and historic resources. Baringer said Sylvan helped to lay the groundwork for many state preserves by working quietly with landowners to explain the significance of their property, and to allay fears that the government might take their land.

With that personable approach Sylvan helped to secure the donation or acquisition of several state preserves, said former state ecologist Dean M. Roosa. Those areas included Mossy Glen, the Bixby addition, and Roggman Boreal Slopes in Clayton County; Mericle Woods in Tama County; and Dinesen Prairie in Shelby County.

Sylvan patiently pointed out to sympathetic landowners and skeptics alike that natural areas could contain "keys to survival" for the human race. Many medicines have been derived from plants and animals, he said. And scientists need undisturbed areas to study the relationships in natural communities. "If we keep destroying these natural areas, we may have lost the ball game," Sylvan said.

"Sy was clairvoyant about the need for natural areas and how they fit into a larger societal framework," Roosa said. What's more, he could persuade others to recognize those connections. "Sy was the consummate interpreter — long before the term 'interpretive naturalist' was coined," Roosa said.

Daryl Smith, a University of Northern Iowa botanist who succeeded Sylvan on the Preserves Board, admired his predecessor's unselfish service. "His ego permitted him to create an idea and give it to someone else," Smith noted. He called Sylvan and Roosa "a dynamic duo" whose contributions to building the state's preserves system can not be overstated.

In 1978 while Sylvan was chairman, the Preserves Board successfully fought off a move to dissolve the board and merge it with other agencies as part of the reorganization of the Iowa Conservation Commission. "We're just a line item in your budget; we know that," Runkel told ICC director Fred Priewert. "Yet we think that the values that the board represents are becoming increasingly important to the people." Other officials agreed, and the Preserves Board escaped the ax.

Although many Iowans knew Sylvan through his work with the Preserves Board and as an SCS biologist in the 1950s, '60s, and early '70s, he became even more involved in conservation activities after

With his trademark ranger's hat, walking stick, camera, Sierra cup, Philmont Scout Ranch jacket, and red plaid shirt, Sylvan posed for this portrait in 1978, in honor of his Oak Leaf Award from The Nature Conservancy. (PHOTO BY LARRY A. STONE)

his retirement. With his public television appearances, books, lectures, and nature hikes, the name "Sylvan Runkel" became synonymous with "conservation" to many Iowans.

He joked with forester friends about his affiliation with the Sierra Club, which has opposed certain logging practices. Sylvan loved to tell the story about the forester who impulsively joined the Sierra Club after he realized that he was about to die. "Better one of them than one of us!" the old ranger told a comrade.

From 1972 to 1974 Sylvan served as president of the Des Moines Audubon Society, a group devoted as much to environmental protection as to studying birds. When hunters advocated opening a mourning dove season in Iowa, many Audubon members opposed the idea. Sylvan, who had been an avid duck and pheasant hunter for many years, tip-toed around the dove-hunting issue. He did not object to most hunting and believed that a hunter "becomes a part of the way the community is working." But Sylvan felt that the emotional debate on dove hunting detracted from more important issues and "wasn't worth the fuss," Bernie said later.

Occasionally Sylvan did enter the fray to lobby actively for environmental causes. He championed public protection for Brown's Woods along the Raccoon River in West Des Moines. He also spoke out against a proposed hog confinement operation adjacent to Steele Prairie State Preserve near Larrabee, Iowa. Those efforts paid off. Polk County now owns Brown's Woods, and the hog facility was relocated.

Whatever the issue, Sylvan always preached the importance of conservation education. Even his first attempts at windbreak planting and erosion control with CCC crews had depended on landowner education. In 1938 he was chosen to head a new SCS program of continuing education for farmers in southwest Iowa, where he worked at the agency's Greenfield office.

Sylvan's SCS boss, State Conservationist Frank Mendell, supported Sylvan's efforts for education, even though Mendell could have insisted that Sylvan stick to traditional soil conservation. With that encouragement, Sylvan proposed an emphasis on "the multitude of interrelationships which exist between the soil, the plants in that soil, and the animal and insect life. Man himself in planning for the fullest use of the land must of necessity work with all of the existing soils, plants, animals, insects, birds, bacteria, etc.," Sylvan wrote in a memo to Mendell.

Sylvan spoke at the 1988 dedication of Hayden Prairie State Preserve, which was named for Ada Hayden, one of his college professors. In the background are prairie enthusiasts Daryl Smith of the University of Northern Iowa (left) and Paul Christiansen of Cornell College.

Another SCS colleague, the late Edwin G. Crocker of Storm Lake, shared Sylvan's passion for conservation education and served with him on the board of the Iowa Chapter of The Nature Conservancy. Crocker thanked his friend "Runk" for introducing him to *A Sand County Almanac* by Aldo Leopold. Following Leopold's lead, the two men organized workshops and public programs that stressed the close links between wildlife and agriculture.

Sylvan strove to emphasize such "connections." He even managed to tie

SYLVAN T. RUNKEL

Einstein's theory of relativity to the folk-saying, "You can't put your foot into the same river twice."

"That's what is happening in nature," Sylvan explained, taking liberty with Einstein's ideas on matter and forces in the environment. "Continuously moving particles, plants growing, wind, water moving, climate changing, decomposing of plants, activity of bacteria — insects — fungi — birds — animals — and our own human activities — always changing — moving."

And don't forget the human element. "Outdoor communities attract people!" Sylvan wrote. "Perhaps it's because way back in the dim and ancient past, we were a natural part of those woodlands and prairies. They were our homes. Our spirits are renewed — we feel happier and more at peace with nature and our fellow man! — when we're in the great outdoor community."

Sylvan sometimes lamented people's decreasing contact with the land. "You're as close to your environment as the next breath you take," he said. "But civilization has gotten away from the real facts of life. When 90 percent of people live in cities, who looks after the conservation of our outdoors? We've got to educate them to real resource conservation."

Even when he was giving a serious talk about environmental problems, Sylvan couldn't resist throwing in a little humor. Noting that the world is growing increasingly polluted, he rhetorically asked who was causing the problem.

"You are! I am! He is! She is!" he declared. Then he paused. "Sounds like I'm conjugating a verb, doesn't it," he quipped. We may have been our own worst enemies, Sylvan dryly admitted. "We were the kinds of kids our mothers didn't want us to play with."

Sylvan's quiet yet sincere defense of nature and wild areas, coupled with his focus on people and private lands in conservation efforts, earned plaudits from a variety of groups. In 1965 he was named Iowa Civil Servant of the Year for his SCS work. The SCS also awarded Sylvan certificates of merit in 1961 and 1972.

In 1967 Sylvan received the Iowa Wildlife Federation's "Conservationist of the Year" award, qualifying him to compete against other state winners for the national title. He lost narrowly to Ed Dodd, creator of the popular "Mark Trail" syndicated newspaper comic strip about the outdoors.

In 1973 the Iowa Chapter of The Wildlife Society named Sylvan to its

Conservation Hall of Fame. He helped to organize the group of wildlife biologists and had served as its president. As president of the Iowa Chapter, Sylvan lobbied for better pay and working conditions for state employees in the field of conservation.

In 1992 the Iowa Natural History Association named a new research scholarship after Sylvan and Roosa. In 1994 the Iowa Natural Heritage Foundation, a private land conservation and resource protection group, gave Sylvan their Lawrence and Eula Hagie Heritage Award.

Sylvan was an honorary life member of the Iowa Association of Naturalists and the Iowa Conservation Education Council. He was a fellow of the Iowa Academy of Science, the Soil Conservation Society of America, and the Society of American Foresters. He was inducted into Gamma Sigma Delta, Iowa State University's honorary society for agriculture.

Sylvan received additional citations from an array of groups, including the Iowa Chapter of the Society of American Foresters, the Iowa Association of Soil Conservation District Commissioners, the Iowa Association of County Conservation Boards, and the National Society of Daughters of the American Revolution.

With all his awards, however, Sylvan received little public recognition for his earnest philosophy of treading lightly on the planet. While with the SCS he often rode a city bus — or sometimes even walked — the five miles from his home to the Federal Building in downtown Des Moines. Occasionally Sylvan would persuade his whole family to walk more than two miles to church, or to Merle Hay Mall for a meal at Bishop's Cafeteria.

In the mid-1970s Sylvan bought a Chevette, a compact car promoted for its fuel economy. Although Bernie was skeptical of the small vehicle, Sylvan wanted to make a statement about conserving resources. His also disdained the disposable, plastic foam cups often used at meetings, preferring instead to bring his own metal Sierra cup, which hung by its wire handle from his belt.

Sylvan served as a good example for conservationists, said Bruce Hopkins, administrator for the Western Hills Area Education Agency, which sponsors the Loess Hills Prairie Seminar. "His eloquence on the natural community in the softest and gentlest of ways reminds all of us of our responsibility as citizens in the world community. He made the connections that provided meaning for living in this natural community. He held us responsible without ever lecturing us."

CHAPTER 18

THE TEACHER

"HE COULD OPEN PEOPLE'S EYES TO WHAT WAS THERE."

Sylvan never stopped teaching. He mentored young friends in his Moline Scout troop and at his church's vacation Bible school. His inquisitive mind and sense of humor rubbed off on his fellow high school and college students. As a CCC camp superintendent, he taught conservation as he learned it — on the land. In the Army Air Corps his passion for flying made him a respected glider pilot instructor. After the horrors of D-Day his example helped other troops to learn the toughness

At Starr's Cave Nature Center in Burlington, Sylvan led one of his typical nature hikes to help people "get acquainted" with natural communities. (Photo by Jean C. Prior)

and love of life they needed to survive. As a father, he taught his children patience and commitment.

During his SCS career and in his retirement, Sylvan taught thousands of conservation workshops for fellow employees and for teachers. He spoke at church meetings, schools, 4-H clubs, garden clubs, civic organizations, county conservation boards, and other groups. But most of all Sylvan was dedicated to teaching kids — to helping them to get acquainted with the natural world.

One of his favorite "classrooms" was Camp EWALU, near Strawberry Point, Iowa. Former camp director John Walledom often watched Sylvan interact with the campers, and he became good friends with the naturalist.

"I remember the first time I met him," said Walledom with a chuckle. He still can picture Sylvan with his walking stick, ranger hat, Sierra cup, camera, and plaid shirt, surrounded by eager children. "I knew this was a guy I wanted to get to know," Walledom said. He tagged along on Sylvan's hikes and grew even more impressed with the Runkel mystique — "the way Sy conducted himself and how he dressed and how he spoke and how he felt in tune with the outdoors."

"He would listen for a bird, or he would pick up a weed, or he'd pick up a branch, and those kids would be right around him," Walledom said. "And then he'd explain a little bit about the woods and about the environment and about caring for the native creatures — and they would listen. And I would look over sometimes at the teachers, and they would be listening just like the kids. He was a storyteller," Walledom said.

Young or old, his listeners were enchanted. "He could make the dust seem interesting," asserted one teacher, who watched Sylvan weave his spell over a group of restless adolescents.

At EWALU Sylvan grew fond of the camp dog, a mutt named Ma. The dog often followed the students on field trips, where Sylvan used the animal to pose a question: "Why is that dog running down the street?" The answer, of course, was: "Because the sun is shining."

Succinctly, Sylvan would point out how life itself depends on photosynthesis. "Every move you make, you are using energy from the sun that came to you by way of the chlorophyll in green plants," he said. "We are actually eating a little chunk of solidified sunlight."

Parents marveled at Sylvan's impact on their children, Walledom said. "Who was that guy that took them on hikes?" the adults wondered. "My son is still talking about him — still talking about what he learned and what he saw, and this kind of elderly fellow... he had this hat... "

"And I'd say, 'Well, that's Sy Runkel,'" Walledom smiled. "He's a special person."

Sylvan showed a genuine interest in the camp and its programs and never failed to thank Walledom for the chance to come to EWALU. He sometimes offered management suggestions, such as placing log steps across trails to slow erosion, and was pleased to see the work completed when he next visited.

When logging was proposed at EWALU, Walledom asked Sylvan's advice. With his forester's insight, Sylvan spelled out the options, explaining how young trees would quickly replace the large ones that were cut, and how some walnut logs would bring a good price. Then he walked through the woodland, suggesting that loggers spare some special trees, like a prominent oak near the dining hall.

Sylvan and Walledom shared quiet moments at Solitude Rock, which rose above one of the camp trails. "We kind of had to climb around and get up there 15 feet or so and then we could look out over the Maquoketa River," Walledom recalled. "And then he would point out the spring beauty and the bloodroot and a few of the other spring flowers and the ferns. He enjoyed me asking him questions. And he'd say, 'That's good, John, that's good.'"

Like most good educators, Sylvan taught by example. People tended to emulate Sylvan's sincere respect for his environment. "If he saw a flower, he would bend down and very tenderly finger the petals and stamens as he looked at the flower. It was almost a reverent position that he was in," observed Sylvan's close friend, the late Jack Borg.

Chris Adkins, now a naturalist for the Dallas County Conservation Board, first heard Sylvan speak on a warm summer evening at Lake Red Rock, with mosquitoes swarming around the audience. "But people were captivated" by Sylvan's program, Adkins remembered. "They stayed and listened. They didn't even swat."

Bill Gilbert, a biology professor at Simpson College in Indianola, said Sylvan's teaching style didn't fit the stereotype of naturalists who try to entertain people with fast-moving, animated presentations. "He would stay in one place for a long time, talking in monosyllables," Gilbert said. But Sylvan's storytelling held his audience spellbound.

"He just had an aura about him," said Gilbert. "It made you pay attention. People would gather in close and listen intently." When they were with Sylvan, they sensed that the environment was "something sacred."

Sacred, perhaps — but not somber. Sylvan liked to find a trail where he could shout out the names of his favorite plants: "RATTLESNAKE" fern in the woods, or "RATTLESNAKE" master on the prairie, or "WAHOO" tree along a fencerow. He would approach the plant while talking quietly, then grin with delight when his outburst startled his companions.

"You were always laughing" on a hike with Sylvan, said Jean Wheeler of Des Moines. Wheeler participated in several of Sylvan's Loess Hills field trips and was so enthralled that she invited him to her wedding. He returned the compliment by attending the ceremony, much to Wheeler's astonishment and delight. When she saw Sylvan among the guests, she screamed for joy.

His sensitivity for people and the environment, coupled with his real enjoyment of the natural world, typified Sylvan's approach to teaching, said retired University of Northern Iowa biology professor Bernard "Ben" Clausen. He worked with Sylvan at the Iowa Teachers Conservation Camp, where Sylvan taught for 24 years, from 1952 to 1975. Sylvan usually led the first field trip, setting the tone for the two- or three-week session.

"His role was to introduce the members of the community so people could get a feel for the totality of the community," Clausen said. "He communicated that so beautifully — the strength of his feelings about these plants. He really cared about them, and it showed in all the field trips he led with teachers. They couldn't help but increase their own awareness and feeling toward nature because of

On prairie hikes, Sylvan looked for rattlesnake master flowers so he could startle his companions with a shout of "RATTLESNAKE!"

contact with him." But Sylvan was more than just a flower-lover or tree-hugger, Clausen added. "He also cared about people. He didn't just care about plants. He was a caring person."

Sylvan was exhilarated by the small natural wonders he would show people on his nature hikes. "We used the same trail every time for the teacher camp, but there were always some surprises," Clausen said. "Every time he'd take a group out, it was an adventure. He would develop the sense of discovery as we went along. And he had stories for everything. You also have to be, to some extent, an actor in order to be a good naturalist," Clausen noted. The teachers never forgot the image of the gentle man with a ranger hat, leaning on his walking stick as he talked of the "fellow citizens" along the trail. "I think Sylvan enjoyed creating the character," Clausen reflected. "And it did help communicate his message."

Sylvan's message endured beyond the teachers' short stay at the workshop, Clausen said. "The teachers went back home enthused, stimulated, and eager to use the information they'd gained at the camp. It carried over into their teaching. And their students got the benefit of it and carried it home. I think it's had quite an effect."

The teachers also learned to have fun, Clausen added. "After the day's work, Sylvan would go in and play on that awful piano that we had. And he would belt out his honky-tonk repertoire, and then we would kind of gather around the fire in the fireplace. We'd have a grand songfest." When the music stopped, Sylvan would tell stories and reminisce about his hitchhiking or mountain-climbing adventures.

For many teachers, Sylvan was the highlight of the camp. "His impact was on a positive attitude toward the environment," Clausen said. "He had so much feeling toward it. When you're working with environmental concerns, it's easy to get discouraged," Clausen admitted, "yet he kept looking positively."

That legacy stands out in the minds of some of Iowa's best teachers, who credit Sylvan Runkel with teaching them. "You have the greatest calling… to help people get acquainted with 'Nature' — the woods — prairie — hills — mountains — marshes — with the natural community that's been here thousands of years," Sylvan once told a group of teacher-naturalists.

Ray Mitchem, who earned the 1973 Junior High Science Teacher of the Year award from the Iowa Hawkeye Science Fair, had just started teaching when he met Sylvan in 1968 at an Iowa Conservation Education Council workshop. He was fascinated with Sylvan's stories of so many "connections" in nature. "He was the old sage; I was the young teacher," said Mitchem, who now teaches earth science and biology at Marshalltown High School. "Before ecology was popular, Sylvan put it to life. He made it real."

Roger Q. "Jake" Landers, a former Iowa State University botany professor who helped to build Iowa's prairie preservation movement, first met Sylvan on a 1962 field trip at Kalsow Prairie. Sylvan had a story for "every plant, insect, soil mound, bird, and natural object," Landers said. Landers especially recalls Sylvan's fondness for prairie crab apples, which he sometimes would pick and carry in his pocket so he could savor the fragrance. Landers considered Sylvan to be "the champion on natural history of Iowa. He impressed me as an enthusiastic, self-taught naturalist who knew more than anyone I'd met."

Landers was a founder of the Iowa Chapter of The Nature Conservancy, and he served with Sylvan on a number of committees and boards, including the Iowa Conservation Education Council. He praised Sylvan's unpretentious leadership. "He was always a voice of quiet optimism that kept us on the track of conservation through education," Landers said. "I know of nobody who had more influence on conservation education of youth in those years than Sylvan Runkel."

Perhaps Sylvan made such a good teacher because he "related so well to ordinary people, and he always had time to talk," said Jean C. Prior, senior research geologist for the Iowa DNR. She met Sylvan at a workshop in the 1960s and later served with him on the State Preserves Advisory Board. "There wasn't anything bureaucratic about Sylvan!" she said with a laugh. His piano playing at meetings also served as a good icebreaker, Prior added. "Music makes everybody feel energized and good!"

Duane Toomsen, retired environmental education coordinator for the Iowa Department of Education, often tapped Sylvan to lead teacher workshops and hikes. Sylvan hooked people not only with his knowledge, but also with the mystery he sometimes wove into his stories. He made people think, Toomsen said.

Sylvan always was willing and eager to help, even when his health had begun to fail. "He would still insist that he was able to participate," Toomsen said. "I knew he could not run out of things to talk about. He'd never go more than 100 yards down the trail — he never got to the end — before the session time had expired."

Sylvan stored a wealth of natural history information in his head —

Students of all ages usually overcame any apprehension when Sylvan shared his fascination with snakes. In 1976 he photographed this class from Orange City, Iowa, getting acquainted with a bullsnake.

but if he ever needed a reference, he usually turned first to *Fieldbook of Natural History*, a 1949 guide by E. Laurence Palmer. He kept one battered copy in his office, one in his den, and one in his Minnesota cabin. Rubber bands held the books together so the dried flowers, pressed leaves, and scribbled notes didn't fall out.

Television producer Tom Moore admired Sylvan's gift for telling stories that introduced his audience to the wonders of nature. "He's with 6- or 7-year-old kids, and suddenly they understand," said Moore. "When they look at a tree, they compare it to a water tower. How does it get water all the way up there?"

Or Sylvan might talk about how fungi dispose of the "garbage" of a natural community. "Fungi being the recyclers, the garbagemen of the woods — that is so brilliant in its own way," Moore said. "It's so simple."

Moore compared Sylvan's philosophies to the "land ethic" of noted conservationist Aldo Leopold. "Very simple, but very deep," Moore said. "No matter how old they are — any kid or any 90-year-old person — they're going to get hooked when they go through what it is that Sylvan is trying to tell them. You're entranced when you're there with him."

As Moore edited videotapes of Sylvan leading a nature hike with a group of youngsters, his respect for Sylvan grew even more. "That whole wildlife walk with Sylvan is absolutely golden," he said. "You'll see some expressions on those kids' faces that show they look at something and know that they were looking at it in a way that they had never looked at it before," Moore said. "You know, that's magic!"

Sylvan's daughter Prasannata heads a Montessori school, which practices the same sort of hands-on teaching that Sylvan used. "It's not just the teacher and the student, it's teacher-environment-student, so you put things in the environment for the child to work with," Prasannata explained. "That's what Dad did when he taught. There was always a concrete thing you could see and learn from. And it was with nature — and life. He could see it and taste it and feel it and share it with everyone. He could open people's eyes to what was there."

Sylvan believed that education works best when "people can see it out there. Feel it and smell it, touch it, get ahold of it. You really don't get it unless you get out there and get your hands in the dirt and touch the leaves and smell the smells of the woods or prairie or marsh, and see the colors," he said. "You become part of it. And that's the way it should be."

Tom Bruegger, director of the Monona County Conservation Board, who worked with Sylvan at the Loess Hills Prairie Seminar, described him as "the consummate teacher. He was humble, gentle, knowledgeable, and he always gave of himself. "One of his greatest abilities was to explain things on a level that the inexperienced would understand," Bruegger said. "He continually compared the natural world with a world we all knew. He humanized, which made things very understandable. There wasn't anything on Earth that wasn't his friend.... Every plant had a use."

Mark Brogie, who teaches junior high and high school science in Creighton, Nebraska, also noted Sylvan's enthusiasm. "He was just excited about everything," Brogie said. "No matter how many times he'd been asked the same question, he always took the time to answer."

On his hikes Sylvan would tell people to look down at the plants. "A lot of people's reaction was that it all looked alike," said Steve Green, former director of Living History Farms. "But he kept encouraging them to look closer and closer until they saw the differences. Invariably, people would be able to identify at least one species of plant they'd been looking at for their whole life and had never seen," Green said. "They always amazed themselves."

SYLVAN T. RUNKEL

Sylvan's goal was to help people to learn — not to show off his own vast knowledge, Green said. "The emphasis was on you, not him," he added. "He taught you to understand it and to learn it and then it was something you had... something you now knew. You felt good about yourself and what you had learned," Green said. "He had a way of not just teaching, but to make you honestly interested in it."

Sylvan let his young students explore the woods, play in the mud, or wade in creeks, Green noted. He recalled Sylvan's response to a 5-year-old climbing a tall tree. He didn't scold the youngster but gently reminded him of the consequences. "If you fall out, you're probably gonna hit the ground hard... probably bounce a couple of times," Sylvan observed.

"He wasn't shocked," Green said. "It seemed perfectly ordinary to him to let those kids take those risks. There was never reprimand. There wasn't this fussiness that the responsible thing to do is make the kids stand on the path with the rest of us."

Naturalist Kirk Henderson of Cedar Falls revered Sylvan so much that he was too shy to ask his idol to autograph a wildflower guide. But Henderson's young daughter eagerly presented the book to Sylvan for his signature. "He could put the adult in awe," Henderson remarked later, "yet the 9-year-old was perfectly at ease with him."

Sylvan sometimes challenged teachers to emulate "the Socrates connection," based on the axiom among educators that "Socrates on a log is better than the finest university." With a natural area as a "log," and a caring teacher as "Socrates," people will learn to understand their role in the environment, Sylvan said.

"What do you see when you go into any natural area?" he asked. "Trees — a forest — a pond — a stream — a scenic valley? But do you see the real, wonderful working of nature? Do you see the natural community? Do you see the citizens? Do you see the work they are doing and how they cooperate for the good of the whole community? A dynamic, progressing panorama of life is going on. It's never the same, but it's continuous," Sylvan asserted.

"These are things that make a walk in the woods, a picnic, a fishing trip, a bird hike, a hunting expedition, or a class trip all worth while," Sylvan wrote. "And they help to point out how we fit in to our surroundings — perhaps help us to see how we belong, and help our understanding of our place on Earth."

In 1996 the Iowa Department of Natural Resources dedicated a 330-acre tract of the Loess Hills Wildlife Area near Turin as the Sylvan Runkel State Preserve.

SYLVAN T. RUNKEL

CHAPTER 19

THE SPIRIT

HE IS HAPPIEST WHO HATH THE POWER
TO GATHER WISDOM FROM A FLOWER.
MARY HOWITT

More than a century ago, Philip Johnson and his Utopian followers built a most unusual church in New Harmony, Indiana. The building wasn't much different from other structures in the town except for one thing: The church had no roof.

Sylvan Runkel admired that unique little church — and he loved what it must have symbolized for the worshippers. "They didn't want anything to separate them from direct heavenly communications from above," he surmised.

Sylvan also praised the Utopians' simple philosophy, which remains etched in a stone in New Harmony's Tillich Park:

Man and nature belong together —
In their created glory —
In their tragedy —
And in their salvation.

"I think that about says it all," Sylvan said. "God — or the Great Spirit–Life Force of Nature — did not create Man and Nature to be separated," he wrote. "They belong together." That was the foundation of Sylvan's quiet, deep spirituality. He saw one community embracing people, a great life force, and nature.

Father Robert W. Kem, retired pastor at St. Andrews Episcopal Church in Des Moines and Sylvan's next-door neighbor for several years, respected his friend's beliefs. "He had depth that a lot of people don't have in terms of trust that things were going to work out all right, and there was a Great Spirit in charge of things, and the spirit manifested itself through nature," Kem said.

Sylvan's reverence for the world around him impressed Bill Darby, a fellow Boy Scout leader. Darby was struck by how much Sylvan's religion was independent of any church service or church building. "I think Sy firmly believed that you could be as close to God as you're ever going to be sitting right here on top of this mountain," Darby said, recalling their time together with Scouts on wilderness backpacking trips.

In his naturalist talks Sylvan often mentioned "the great master builder who created our universe and our world." He spoke of "the miracle of life" in the context of chlorophyll, which he called "the foundation of creation." And he liked to remind people that the hemoglobin molecules in their blood differ from the chlorophyll in plants by only one atom. Hemoglobin has an iron atom where chlorophyll has a magnesium atom. This shows the intimate relationship between people and plants, Sylvan concluded. "We are more closely related to the plants than you might think," he said. He reverently referred to "the original spark of life" that links all living things to the beginnings of life on Earth.

"Each one of us shares in holding onto that original spark of life for the duration of his life cycle, after which each one of us is taken back again into that great basic life source from which all life continually emanates," said Sylvan in a eulogy for his good friend and coauthor, Al Bull.

Sylvan couldn't be content to just accept the concept of "that great basic life source," however. His scientist's curiosity demanded that he ask one more question. "Who or what made the plants start this the first time?" he wondered. "It would appear that there is a great inner intelligent life force which is within every living thing, and that whatever is needed to meet and solve problems will gradually, in time, evolve successfully, for the life form and for the community." He left it up to the listener to decide whether that "great inner intelligent life force" should be called God, Allah, or simply the Great Spirit.

When his son Ramon was preparing to become a Lutheran minister, Sylvan quizzed him intently, urging Ramon to consider the implications of entering the seminary. But Sylvan also discussed the need for people to look beyond the material world. "You really have to get a hold of something that is far bigger than you are," Sylvan told Ramon. "You really have to find a sense of greater value and greater connection, or else life can be pretty miserable."

As much as he respected those "values" or "connections" or "the old master who got life started on this planet," however, Sylvan did not simply accept religious doctrine. Instead, he frequently contemplated the relationships and forces that link the spiritual and natural worlds. "He had such respect for the natural order of things," Ramon said.

While Ramon was a student and after he became ordained, he and Sylvan continued those lively philosophical discussions. "Dad was able to offer some questions I had a hard time answering or addressing," Ramon admitted.

Sylvan's stories sometimes moved listeners to ponder their own spiritual beliefs. He often told about the park ranger who was vividly describing how Nature made the wonders of the Grand Canyon, how Nature had carved the chasm, how Nature had created the lovely colors.

"What about God?" demanded a tourist. "Didn't He have anything to do with it?"

The ranger drew a line on a paper with his pen, then asked whether he, or the pen, had made the mark. "Did Mother Nature make that Grand

Sylvan photographed this bunchberry (dwarf dogwood), which was one of his favorite wildflowers, near his cabin in northern Minnesota.

Canyon, or did the great living life force that is within, around, and about — that some people call God — did God make it?" the ranger wondered. "You can't separate the two. We see Nature working — but we don't see the Great Spirit behind it!"

As children, Sylvan and his two sisters, Geneva and Dorothy, regularly attended the Union Congregational Church in Moline. But Sylvan spent more time marveling at the wonders of Earth than he did studying liturgy. "Nature and things that grew were more important to him than the rituals," Geneva said. "Sylvan didn't think of it as 'religion.' It was the way of life."

It's not surprising, therefore, that Sylvan is conspicuously absent from a 1922 photograph of vacation Bible school students he and Geneva were helping to teach at the church. Sylvan had taken his young companions out into the woods, where they could get closer to "the great master builder." After all, he asserted, "the groves or natural woodlands were the first temples, or churches."

Sylvan often spoke and wrote with reverence about his beloved woods and prairies. And he cherished what he called the "accumulated wisdom" of other people who were close to the earth. He liked to quote a Nigerian chieftain: "I conceive that the land belongs to a great family of people. Many are dead, a few are living, and a vast number are still unborn."

Despite their diversity, many religions share this common belief about how the "spark of life" continues through all living communities, Sylvan observed. He pondered the Hindu philosophy that the world is "always becoming." But he stressed that people, who are a part of its natural communities, also shape what that world becomes.

"It is only when we realize we are part of something God-given, with the responsibility toward it, that we can understand, love, and respect the land, which gives us not only our food, but also our culture," Sylvan said. If we believe, to whatever degree, that the world is somehow the creation of "the great master builder," then it becomes our spiritual obligation to care for the earth, Sylvan asserted. But, unfortunately, that obligation may be a concept that some modern religions and societies ignore, he suggested.

"In the rush toward progress, or so-called progress," he wrote, "often times we are disorganizing the land much faster than we are appreciating the natural community and our dependence on it. This lack of appreciation, or simply ignorance, is one of the most destructive forces in the world."

By teaching us to look more closely at our communities, and to recognize our own shortcomings, perhaps Sylvan was helping us conquer the "destructive forces" that could be our downfall. He occasionally quoted the Bible, Revelation 7:3, which offers pointed advice on caring for the Earth: "Hurt not the earth, neither the sea, nor the trees."

One of Sylvan's favorite Native American proverbs puts it even more bluntly: "The frog does not drink up the pond in which he lives."

If only people would learn more about the "pond" that is their home, then they would try harder to protect it, Sylvan believed.

In his own subtle way Sylvan tried to demonstrate that universal connection between people and nature, and to help people appreciate their surroundings and their fellow citizens. Through his books, his nature hikes, his TV appearances, his Boy Scout outings, his slide programs, his casual conversations, Sylvan exuded a contagious sense of wonder about the world.

He often quoted a short verse by Mary Howitt:

He is happiest who hath the power
To gather wisdom from a flower.

A Loess Hills wildflower hike with Sylvan became a spiritual renewal for farmer/poet Michael Carey of Farragut, Iowa. "I knew that I was in the presence of a legend," Carey said. "What he communicated was a sense of wonder and a reverence for the trees and plants around us. In the end, he waxed rhapsodic about light, and leaves and chlorophyll. How the trees are huge photosynthetic machines and how we more indirectly are as well... how we are all light, in a sense, incarnate. The class was a religious experience as much as a scientific one," Carey recalled.

"After I listened to him, it was easy to see how the early human societies became sun worshippers, and saw God as a great blinding light.

"Through Sy I came to understand more intimately how God is shining all around us and through us," Carey added. "The prairie and the forest now seem to me like churches. Ones that God made for us to celebrate Him (or Her or It) and worship in."

Some people might be tempted to call Sylvan an evangelist for the protection of natural resources. He avoided such labels, however. When pressed, he'd suggest with a grin that he was simply "an old forester." But Sylvan graciously accepted a tribute from an SCS colleague, Ivan T.

Salmons of Charles City, Iowa: "Your greatest contribution to society has been your ability to cause people to have reverence for this great wonderful world in which we are privileged to live," Salmons said.

For Sylvan's children, lessons about that wonderful world also included attending church regularly. But their father did not demand adherence to a strict ideology, noted Jon. Sylvan primarily expected the youths to show their esteem for the world.

Prasannata found a special meaning in her father's reverence. "I heard about the cycle of life ever since I was a little bitty kid," she recalled. "Everything is related and connected. There is a world 'oneness,' a world people."

Prasannata also took to heart Sylvan's belief that we share the world with "fellow citizens," which we should respect and learn from. "He loved every little plant and every little creature," Prasannata said. She has tried to live by that example in a "world community" made up of individual concerned citizens. "The only way you can have peace is to have it inside you and offer it to a friend," she said.

Perhaps, as Sylvan was trying to help others understand the larger natural order, he also was leading them to look inward to their own spirituality. The science of life and the universe — from energy cycles to

Sylvan's six children gathered to help him celebrate his 88th birthday August 1994. From left: Front – Bernie and Sylvan. Middle – Jeff, Jon, Tom. Rear – Prasannata, Marilyn Runkel Hemstad, Ramon.

SYLVAN T. RUNKEL

nitrogen cycles — might not fit with traditional religious teachings, Sylvan realized. But he proposed that these conflicts could be resolved by assuming that there is a "spiritual life force, which is in full control." If we acknowledge a "great all-powerful spirit," maybe it doesn't matter whether we call that spirit "God."

Even as his life was nearing its end in January 1995, Sylvan continued to ponder those questions. Sylvan did not express a fear of death; rather, he remained intensely curious about the natural process. "What's the next step?" he asked his pastor. "Can you tell me?" The cleric paused, then turned the query back to Sylvan. "I don't know," he admitted. "But maybe you can teach us, Sylvan."

Indeed, for many years, Sylvan had been gently, subtly urging people to contemplate "the next step." He may have spoken most passionately when he eulogized friends who had shared his view of the inseparable links between man and nature. For example, he praised the late Manford Ellerhoff, a northeast Iowa forester:

"His memory is in the hearts and minds of everybody who knew him — and everybody who knew him is the better for it!" Sylvan said. "To me, he is part of every Iowa woodland — a part of that very real, but unseen life force which keeps it going!"

At the dedication of Hayden Prairie State Preserve in Howard County, Sylvan imagined the spirit of Ada Hayden, his former botany professor, still exploring the Iowa prairies. Hayden's great respect for the land and her dedication to prairies had inspired Sylvan as a young Iowa State College forestry student more than 60 years before.

"Wherever there are wild prairie grasses and flowers — where there is the song of the restless wind on the tallgrass prairie — there Ada Hayden will find her eternal home," he said. Sylvan may have been contemplating his own future, dreaming of an afterlife shared with his "fellow citizens"; of endless hikes to discover coneflowers, smell wild roses, climb mountains, or hear waves crash on the lakeshore. He likened death to an exciting journey over the mountains, rather than an end to life.

"I have long suspected that when we finally cross the Big Range, we will use this Earth as our home," Sylvan said, "and what we do to it now will determine whether it will be heaven or hell!"

Sylvan climbed the Loess Hills of western Iowa to photograph this yucca, which is characteristic of the dry prairie slopes.

SYLVAN T. RUNKEL

EPILOGUE

By Jon W. Stravers

During the last two years of his life I was able to visit Sylvan six or seven times. I knew him from his activities with The Nature Conservancy and the Iowa State Preserves Board, and I had learned a great deal about him through my friendship with Dean Roosa. Sylvan and Dean were partners in conservation for more than 20 years. Dean, who encouraged me to talk with Sylvan, had guided and mentored my work during the initial years of my raptor research in Iowa. Dean often spoke of Sylvan's commitment and connection to the land, his unique personal history, and his ability to communicate with landowners about conservation. My father, Tony, also influenced me to initiate this contact with Sylvan. Tony always had taken time to visit and help care for important people in his life, especially when they were ill or when they reached their declining years.

Sometimes my visits with Sylvan lasted for most of an afternoon or on into the evening. Other visits were brief, but during all of them we talked extensively about a variety of Sylvan's experiences. We often talked about conservation issues. More specifically, we discussed connections to the earth and to the universe through members of natural communities such as skunk cabbage, red-shouldered hawks, and swamp white oaks, with an emphasis on the exploration of wild places.

The passion we both shared for wild places pushed our discussion into places of sheer beauty and excitement. At times, Sylvan's failing health made him temporarily confused about the present. But his mind cleared and his memory sharpened when I would ask about such things as his trip in 1925, or about spending a summer doing a fire watch in a wilderness area out west. Even things like the relationships among reed canary grass, old-growth forests along the Mississippi River, and foraging opportunities for red-shouldered hawks would excite Sylvan's imagination and spawn all kinds of questions. He often brought new meaning to questions that I had been struggling with for 20 years, and to some things that I had known but not put into perspective.

All through these discussions, Sylvan brought the idea that we are more than just our physical selves. We are all that we see; all that flows to us from a thousand natural sources, some noted, some half-noted, some not noted at all, except by some sense that lies too deep for naming. When we are truly connected to the land, then the land actually becomes part of us. Our rhythms are in tune with the seasonal processions; our spirit rises with the rise of a mountain ridge, or flows with the flow of a river.

I remember clearly that Sylvan enjoyed discussing raptor migration as it occurred through our state and region. He had a keen idea about the way all things in the natural world are connected, and he quickly understood how ancient geological features have influenced raptor migration every single autumn for thousands of years. The face of the planet has changed drastically in the last 200 years, especially in Iowa, and raptor populations have changed drastically as a result. Despite human activities that changed the face of the landscape, the ridges and bluffs along the river have always influenced and aided raptor migration. Sylvan loved that idea of the long-term connection between the raptors and the ancient rocks. It made the geological history of our state come alive.

At one point we had a lengthy and excited discussion about the Balltown Escarpment — a Silurian ridge just north of Dubuque that forces the Mississippi River to run east and west for about 20 miles. I told Sylvan that raptors love to hug that ridge and ride the deflected wind currents, since the ridge makes flying easier on some days. Sylvan loved the setting at Balltown and its famous restaurant. This new piece of information about raptors migrating by there made him smile.

Our last visit together was about two weeks before Sylvan died. He knew the end was near, and I could tell the light within him was starting to fade. We talked about the mortality of the physical body and immortality of the spirit. I remember telling him that somewhere someone will keep singing his "Occasional Ode to Loess Hills." But I also told him that he had influenced many of us in our ways of being connected to the planet, and I promised him (without knowing how I was going to do it at the time) that I would keep telling the stories that he had told me. As my friends will tell you, I have been telling Sylvan stories ever since. I can break into one at any particular moment, and I suspect that I will be doing that until I quit telling stories altogether.

When I heard of Sylvan's death, I was saddened — but only briefly. I celebrated his life and spirit, and I also celebrated the fact that I had been able to talk with him before he left us. I felt a richness he had planted within me that death could not take away.

When I attended the family visitation for Sylvan the night before his funeral, I talked with Sylvan's sister Geneva and his oldest daughter, Marilyn. They had been with him during his final hours, and they were discussing some of Sylvan's last words. (This was the first time I had met either of these women, and they had no idea that I had spent the best part of my life studying hawks.) One of the last things Sylvan talked about was Balltown — the Balltown Ridge and the famous restaurant in Balltown. And as they were telling me about it, they said that Sylvan said to them, "And the hawks fly by there, don't they?"

The words puzzled his family — but the instant I heard them, my spirit was riveted. I felt spiritually connected to this incredible human being and the spirit that we called Sylvan Runkel, and I also felt there was something to be done with that connection — something to be shown or revealed.

While I was sure I had received a message, I had absolutely no idea what it meant or how to follow its call. I remember leaving the visitation in somewhat of a daze. But I kept the feelings of being connected to Sylvan alive in my heart and waited for the seeds to sprout.

Fortunately, I had been building a friendship with Sylvan's wife, Bernie. She and two friends, Ida Ruth Miller and Carol Selsor, have a custom of getting together one day each week. They made a couple of trips to the Red Rock Lake area to watch wintering bald eagles with me. It was during these trips that I began to get a better understanding of other aspects of Sylvan's life. I also realized that his story needed to be told.

Although I jumped at the opportunity to write Sylvan's story, I buckled under the sheer weight of a story that covered 88 adventurous years. I turned instinctively to the best writing friend I had, Larry Stone, and since then I have been able to assist him all along the way during this six-year project.

This book is about a personal history, but it covers only a small portion of the story of Sylvan's fascinating life. There are more stories but simply not enough room to tell them. If nothing else, we hope this book shows the beauty of a life connected physically and spiritually to what we call the planet Earth. And we hope Sylvan's spirit will challenge all of us to become better citizens of the natural world.